ALAN PARTRIDGE:
ALPHA PAPA

SCRIPT (AND SCRAPPED)

**STEVE COOGAN, ROB GIBBONS, NEIL GIBBONS,
ARMANDO IANNUCCI & PETER BAYNHAM**

HarperCollins*Publishers*

HarperCollins*Publishers*
1 London Bridge Street
London SE1 9GF

www.harpercollins.co.uk

Published by HarperCollins*Publishers* 2013

A catalogue record of this book is
available from the British Library

ISBN 978-0-00-755823-0

FOREWORD
BY STEVE COOGAN

From the Paris Studios (not in Paris) to
Cromer's Hotel de Paris (also not in Paris)

'Whenever you're ready.' Three simple words uttered by a shortish Scottish man behind a glass screen to a slightly taller man from the north of England. No, not a tight-lipped prison officer to a semi-literate tattooed murderer during visiting time, but a wordsmith/radio producer to a keen young actor/comic in a basement studio on Lower Regent Street. Their names unknown, their faces unremarkable, just like the throngs of shoppers, workers and Japanese tourists taking pointless photos above their heads (on Regent Street).

The young actor/comic known simply as 'Steve' to his friends and 'Coogan' to others would one day become a household name. The Scottish radio producer was known simply as Arm, an arm that extended fully to become Armando Iannucci. Again, a name that would become, not a universal household name, but certainly a name known in households where books and broadsheet newspapers are welcome cohabitees. The date was 6 September 1991, Cool Britannia was still only a twinkle in a mad marketing man's eye, but the assembled band of rogues, misfits and brigands, mostly from Oxford University, were ahead of the curve. The walls of the Paris Studios (not in Paris) were adorned with pictures of radio comedy legends – Tony Hancock,

The Goons, Round the Horn, The Archers – but Armando's repertory of strolling players would join the pantheon with ease.

The Scotsman leaned forward and pressed the intercom button again. 'Steve, in your own time …' The provincially unworldly northern man emptied his mind (no mean feat) and let his body become a kind of subconscious conduit for what was to follow. He cleared his throat and began to speak. 'I'm Alan Partridge.' The rest …

Fast forward to spring 2013. It's a very different world: fat phones and pagers gather dust in kitchen drawers, video tapes lie forgotten in the cardboard-box graveyard of the attic – but one thing survives in this post-9/11 digital apocalypse: Alan Partridge.

The name's on everyone's lips as a nation waits with bated breath for the start of filming. The hushed whispers of anticipation are deafening. School teachers, grocers, armed policemen at Heathrow, DJs, farmers and media-studies students talk frantically about the upcoming film: 'I can't wait for it,' says an unemployed florist; 'I'm going to take my girlfriend,' a man out walking his dog says to a jogger. Online comments are going through the roof: 'It's going to be shit,' says one observer; 'It used to be funny but this'll be shit,' says another; 'How shit do you think it's going to be?' adds a third. But the film was to confound those whingeing twats. 'A quietly audacious triumph', proclaimed the *Guardian*, and 'Better than I thought it was going to be,' said one of those whingeing twats, begrudgingly.

Sorry about the first five paragraphs. I sort of started off ironic then got sidetracked into getting stuff off my chest. So I will just try and get to 1,500 words talking about *Alpha Papa*, the Alan Partridge movie.

After the second series of *I'm Alan Partridge* (2001) there was a long gap, about 10 years. Armando was tied up with *The Thick of It*, among other things; Pete Baynham had gone to America to write for Sacha Baron Cohen; and I was busy with my production company Baby Cow, and making occasional forays into Michael Winterbottom films. We had talked about doing an Alan film on and off over the years but there didn't seem to be a huge appetite for it, and the chances of getting all of us together to do it were slim to non-existent. Alan has always been a mixed blessing for me: while it meant I was typecast by the role, it also was still with me, and I'd find myself imagining what Alan would say about this or that. Like an old school-friend, I started to wonder what he was up to, what he was doing. All this was academic, though, as without a writing team of the highest calibre to bring him back to life I'd be on my tod, which was too depressing a prospect. Then Rob and Neil Gibbons turned up.

I was doing a live tour in 2008 and asked the non-identical twin brothers from Sandbach if they wanted to have a go at writing something for Alan. When I read their material it was a bit of a Holy Grail moment. I was crying, laughing out loud at stuff that was both detailed and authentic. I remember being a bit shocked at the confidence of their comedic voice. It had a similarity to Arm and Pete's and my style, which of course it was derived from, but it was more rounded and humane. They made the *Daily Mail*-reading little-Englander a bit more likeable! Armando agreed, and their involvement gave new impetus to the character, which was properly realised in *Mid Morning Matters*, the online 10-minute webisodes that allowed us to isolate Alan and get even further inside his head. These were both a way of not repeating ourselves with a TV series and of experimenting with the character in a low-profile environment. Incredibly satisfying, subtle and myopic, they were crowned by the autobiography *I, Partridge: We Need to Talk About Alan*, mostly written by Neil and Rob, with a bit of help from Arm and me. The book was an extremely funny delusional character study, with a big dollop of pathos. It, along with a couple of Sky specials, showed that there was life in the old dog yet ... so we decided to get on with the film.

This was a difficult thing to write and a nightmare to shoot. The Gibbons worked hard but Arm and I were grappling with other projects – Arm on *Veep*, his HBO series, while I was co-writing the screenplay for *Philomena* – so Rob and Neil ended up doing the heavy lifting. The problem we were all trying to solve, though, was how to translate Partridge to the big screen in a way that was cinematic – with a kind of appropriate magnitude – without losing the myopic quality that's part of Alan's DNA. Early ideas, such as al-Qaeda at BBC Television Centre, were deemed too outlandish, while others felt too prosaic, like an overlong TV episode. So we settled on something sort of big but very provincial. The 1975 Sidney Lumet film *Dog Day Afternoon* was a point of reference for us – something amateur but extraordinary – so we don't go to America, Alan doesn't go on holiday, we stay at Alan's radio station in Norwich and a disgruntled ex-DJ (Pat Farrell) takes everyone hostage. We liked the notion of Alan and Pat being yesterday's men, dwarfed by the uncaring media leviathan, but with humanity somehow winning through. Yeah, alright, it's not Franz Kafka; but then *The Trial* isn't hilarious.

We started shooting in February 2013 and the first week was, not to put too fine a point on it, a fucking nightmare.

I had just finished my serious film so hadn't given this one the attention it needed, Arm was being funny 3,000 miles away, and our leading actor had just pulled out 'cos he thought the script was ... well, not very good. As the clock ticked away towards Day One of shooting, and Rob, Neil and I wrestled with the script, the atmosphere became more and more bleak. Declan Lowney, of *Father Ted* and *Little Britain* fame, had agreed to direct but looked like someone who had won a first-class ticket aboard the *Titanic*. If our producer Kevin Loader had brought a revolver along his only dilemma would have been whether to shoot himself – or everyone else, which would've been an act of mercy. And if you think my tired *Titanic* simile and gun hyperbole aren't funny, try rewriting a comedy script in that atmosphere. Anything seemed funnier: *Das Boot*, or even Adam Sandler. We'd shoot for eight or nine hours, then spend a further three or four rewriting the following day's stuff. Some days, with the crew standing round in silence, Declan would look at me with a thousand-yard stare and say, 'Steve, we *need* to shoot something,' and I'd reply, 'Rob and Neil are just printing off the script now; it'll be here in a minute.'

Then we started to get two days ahead with the rewrites, and we started laughing because we saw the dailies and we were getting funny stuff. After that it went from chaos to organised chaos and it became apparent we could make a funny film. It was at times even enjoyable! The crew and my fellow actors showed the patience of saints, Felicity Montagu was sublime, breathing life into Lynn like she had never gone away, and Simon Greenall as Michael added some spice. Tim Key as Sidekick Simon would save our life in the edit, when all we had to do was cut to that complicated face of his to make a scene work. Nigel Lindsay, Phil

Cornwell and Monica Dolan all fleshed out their characters to keep it real, and accommodated my undemocratic nature on set. Even Colm Meaney, who brought depth and pathos to his role as Pat, kept his patience – apart from once during the shoot. 'This is like a fucking student film,' he said. He wasn't wrong.

Steve Coogan
Brighton, 24 October 2013

ALAN PARTRIDGE:
ALPHA PAPA

Note: Dotted lines in the margin indicate that the text was not included in the final screenplay.

EXT. CROMER COAST — DAWN — DAY 1

*It's dawn over Cromer Pier. The mournful music —
'Koyaanisqatsi' by Philip Glass — suggests something
portentous.*

Caption: Norfolk.

INT. RADIO STATION — FOYER — TUESDAY — DAY 1

*Over the same music, fade into a shot panning across
cheesy portrait shots of North Norfolk Digital DJs,
hung on a wall. DAVE CLIFTON, wearing a leather jacket
and Keane T-shirt; WALLY BANTER, a zany Timmy Mallet
type; a mid-twenties female DJ (perhaps doing
something unfunny with a microphone); DANNY SINCLAIR,
trendy haircut man; TONIA SCOTT, a safe, current-
affairs specialist; ALAN PARTRIDGE and PAT FARRELL.
Both Pat and Alan's photos were taken 15 or so years
ago and lack the crispness of digital shots.*

As we pan across, a voice off-camera can be heard
unhelpfully joining in with the singing. It's Alan.

    ALAN
    (Singing)
    'Koyaanisqatsiiiiii' ... Rom-pom-pom-pom ...

A wider shot shows a man, Pat (a folk DJ in DMs),
staring blankly at the photo of his younger self. He's
in the reception area of a small local radio station
and looks troubled.

INT. RADIO STATION – STUDIO – DAY 1

Alan turns the music off quickly and we see he's on
air. SIDEKICK SIMON is sitting beside him.*

    ALAN
    Well, that music was very foreboding! It's made a
    shiver go right down my spine ...

....

* We shot this scene twice. We got some good stuff first time round (on the opening day of the shoot) but it was all quite bitty, when what the scene needed was Alan at the top of his game. We shot it again on the very last day of the shoot, using some of the original material and a fair bit of new stuff. Then we put the best bits of each together in the edit. Finding out we were going to get another go at it, the scene was a bit of a luxury on a shoot devoid of luxuries (excluding the excellent puddings provided by our caterers). If memory serves, at some point between the first and second go at this scene, Tim Key, who plays Simon, had gone and had his hair cut. Unprofessional.

SIMON
That'll be the air conditio—

ALAN
(Ignoring him)
I would have taken it off sooner, but I was having
a fascinating conversation with the proud father of
Norfolk's most suntanned child. Just passed his
details on to the social services. The time is
11:59 and 55 seconds.

SIMON
Midday.

ALAN
No. Well, yes, it is now! You're listening to Mid
Morning Matters.

JINGLE: 'Mid Morning Matters with Alan Partridge,
music and chat for the Norfolk generation.'

The jingle ends with a jazzy keyboard flourish that
Alan mimes, but in the wrong direction.

ALAN (CONT'D)
Sorry, it's the other way, isn't it? Later on we'll
be taking dedications for anyone who's been wrongly
turned down for planning permission. Also, I'll be
asking which is the worst monger: fish, iron,
rumour or war? Pretty clear, that one, but now it's
time for today's Large Question.

JINGLE: Booming voices saying 'Large Question'.

ALAN (CONT'D)
It's the near future and an unprovoked chemical
attack from France or possibly China has left us
without a sense of smell. In a whiff-free world,
what smell would you miss the most?

He puts on an urgent bed of music and takes a breath.

ALAN (CONT'D)
Tom, in Diss.

TOM
(Telephone)
Petrol!

ALAN
Nice! Wrongly and confusingly referred to by the
Americans as gas. It's petrol, not gas. Dominic, in
Castle Acre?

DOMINIC
(Telephone)
Money.

ALAN
Yes. Joe, in Holt.

JOE
(Telephone)
My wife's nightie.

ALAN
You kinky get!

SIMON
Saucy sod!

JOE
(Telephone)
She died, you see.

Awkward pause.

ALAN
Smells matter.

SIMON
They do.

INT. RADIO STATION – RECEPTION – DAY 1

Slippery station manager GREG and big-collared, Range Rover-driving Gordale Media boss JASON enter the reception area. Pat is onto them straight away as if he's been waiting for them.

Alan's show can be heard faintly over the speakers.

PAT
Greg. You know, this is a great station, a real cracker.

GREG
Yes. Hi, Pat. Jason Tresswell, Managing Director of …

PAT
Gordale Media. Our new owners. I googled you on
Yahoo.

GREG
Yes, Pat. Pat Farrell does weeknights, 10 to 12.

PAT
Sleepy-time slot.

JASON
So, are you on your way out?

PAT
You tell me.

*A pregnant pause, unhelpfully broken by the sound of
Alan.*

ALAN
Gillian writes to ask, 'Is it true you're being
taken over by a bunch of corporate whores?'

CUT TO:

INT. RADIO STATION - STUDIO - DAY 1

Alan notices Jason through the window as he speaks.

ALAN
(Less confident)
Gillian, I'm 99 per cent certain that's not true.

SIMON
We've got a text here from Joy, in Diss, who says
an easy way to solve the problems in Israel …

ALAN
Bit thorny.

SIMON
… would be for Judaism and Islam to merge.

ALAN
Yes, wouldn't hold your breath.

SIMON
Well, they both hate pigs.

ALAN
True enough.

SIMON
They could call it Jislam.

*Alan furiously gesticulates at Simon while maintaining
a calm broadcasting voice.*

ALAN
I think you can go in circles, can't you, trying to
think of names for something, even a cat. Well,
nettles cause them, dock leaves cure them. It's a
sting. It's Sting.

He puts on 'Roxanne' by The Police and they're off-air.

SIMON
Sorry.

ALAN
(Livid)
Never, never criticise Muslims! Only Christians.
And Jews a little bit.

*Pat pops his head in, as Alan — off-air — takes a big
mouthful of cake.* He has his back to us. We've not
seen his face.*

PAT
Alan — it's started. They're here. We're being
taken over.

*Alan spins round. The camera slowly pushes in on him
as he chews and chews and chews. By the time he finally
swallows we're tight on him.*

ALAN
So?

....

* On the day we shot this, the three of us [Rob, Neil, Steve] had a pretty
heated discussion about what Alan should be eating here. Cream cake?
Ice cream? An orange? We needn't have bothered – they'd already
bought the cream cakes.

EXT. ROAD – WEDNESDAY – DAY 2

Over the sound of 'Roxanne', we see LYNN trundling along in a beige Mini Metro.

EXT. ALAN'S HOUSE – DAY 2

Establishing shot: Lynn going into Alan's house.

INT./EXT. ALAN'S HOUSE – DAY 2

She can hear him singing in a broad West Indian accent, but there's no sign of him.

ALAN
(Singing, off)
'Coconut, coconut. Everybody like de coconut.
Coconut, coconut …'

LYNN
Hello? Are you in the business centre?

Lynn walks through the kitchen, then it's out of his house and up his back garden towards a large garden shed that Alan uses as his office.

INT. ALAN PARTRIDGE SHED – DAY 2

Alan sits at a desk in the shed, in front of a laptop.

He's wearing glasses and doesn't realise the screen is reflected in them, showing he's looking at porn. An image of a big naked backside takes up each lens.

ALAN
Oh, hello, Lynn. I'm just reading about how ospreys died out in Britain and had to be reintroduced from Scandinavian stock in the early Nineties. And now I think there are almost 500 of them.

He looks at the screen and clicks the mouse, then looks back up with a new porn image filling his glasses.

ALAN (CONT'D)
Yep, 480. It shows we should treasure and value our wildlife.

Lynn grunts in attempted agreement. He shuts the laptop.

ALAN (CONT'D)
So, what you got, girl?

LYNN
Well, the butchers want you to do another voiceover …

ALAN
Bannan's the Butchers, yesterday's meat at today's
prices.*

LYNN
... and you've had the Mayor of Hickling get in
touch. He listens to your show and he wants to
offer you the freedom of the village.

ALAN
Hickling doesn't even have a post office.

LYNN
They give you a big key.

ALAN
How big?

....

* The film was mainly shot in a disused office block in Mitcham (south
London); this was our radio studio set. We then headed to Norwich and
Cromer to do the location stuff, before finishing off in a borrowed house
near Epsom Downs Racecourse to shoot the scenes at Alan's house. We
were rewriting this scene in Cromer late at night after a long day of
filming in sub-zero temperatures on the pier – perfect conditions for
creating high-quality comedy. We were sitting around a big table in the
inappropriately named Hotel de Paris (Rob, Neil, Steve and our terrific
script editor Graham Duff), playing about with different products and
different straplines. We ended up with the authentic-sounding
'Bannan's the Butchers, today's meat at yesterday's prices'. Then, just as
we were about to shoot the scene, we decided to flip it around so we get
an extra joke from Alan's worried look – 'Have they got it wrong or me?'

LYNN
That big.

ALAN
Tell them I accept. Well, everything seems to be
chugging along nicely.

Alan is distracted by a text. He seems perturbed.

LYNN
Everything okay, Alan?

ALAN
Our friend Michael's just sent a text saying he
hasn't bought toilet paper in 18 months.

LYNN
How does he …?

He scrolls down and looks relieved.

ALAN
Ah, he steals it from a pub. That's a relief. I
shared a bag of salty popcorn with him last week.

INT. RADIO STATION - STUDIO 2 - DAY 2

Pat sits in Studio 2, recording a promo for his show.
He looks tired.

PAT
Hi, I'm Pat Farrell. Join me tonight at 10 for a
hearty casserole of tunes, cheer and chinwag. Local
folk trio Will o' the Wisp will be playing live in
the studio and I'll be taking your calls on my
ever-popular fireside phone-in. Don't miss it.

CUT TO:

INT. RADIO STATION - STUDIO 1 - DAY 2

Watching him through the glass are breakfast-show DJ
Danny Sinclair and his posse of twats.

DANNY
Okay, then, well, for those of you who haven't
slipped into a coma, you are listening to the
breakfast show, with me, Danny Sinclair, and this
bunch of muppets.

The posse whoop and holler.

We intercut with Alan driving to work in driving
gloves.

DANNY (CONT'D)
How are we feeling this morning, then, guys?

POSSE MEMBER
Better than you by the looks of things.

DANNY
Oh, excuse me, I had it large. I got on it.

POSSE MEMBER
You need to take it easy tonight, then.

DANNY
Well, I wish I could but we've got the launch,
haven't we, tonight. Because, as you know, North
Norfolk Digital are changing their name to …

He pauses for effect.

DANNY (CONT'D)
'Shape — the way you want it to be.'

*JINGLE: A soulless voice sings, 'Shape — the way you
want it to be.'*

*Meanwhile, Alan reaches a zebra crossing. He sees a
billboard of Danny. He's raising an eyebrow and has
tape over his mouth. The wording says: 'The only way
to shut him up. Breakfast with Danny Sinclair on North
Norfolk Digital.' Alan tuts.*

DANNY (CONT'D)
Coming up next, Alan Partridge, God bless him. I
mean, he's what …?

POSSE MEMBER
How old is he?

DANNY
Sixty or something? He's got to be, hasn't he?

ALAN
I'm 55!

*In the next lane, a bloke in a Range Rover (Jason) is
pissing himself at this, which annoys Alan. As they
pull away, Alan swerves towards the Range Rover. Jason
swerves to avoid Alan, spilling his coffee and crying
out in pain.*

JASON
You dick!

ALAN
(Smug, over his shoulder)
No. You dick!

*Beep! The action cuts back to Alan sitting in traffic
with a faraway look on his face. Jason's gone and
Alan's holding up the traffic — it was a daydream. He
stalls as he moves away and is beeped again.*

ALAN (CONT'D)
A horn's to warn, not rebuke!*

---

* This is taken verbatim from Steve's dad.

DANNY
Oh, Alan, we love you, mate. We love you, really.
This one's for you if you're listening. It's
Roachford.

Danny mimes shooting himself in the head.

As Alan pulls away we see the side of his car for the
first time. In massive writing it reads 'Alan Partridge
Drives This Kia'.

TITLE SEQUENCE*

Alan drives past a 'Welcome to Norwich' sign and is on
the open road.

He mimes along to Roachford's 'Cuddly Toy', absolutely
word perfect, meaning every line. The longer the song
goes on, the more he's giving it the full, swaggering
pop star.

....

* Our original intention had been to shoot a glossy Bond-style title
sequence, with naked silhouettes and slo-mo acrobatics. The girls had
been booked. But a) we were short of time and b) there was a nagging
feeling that a Bond tribute felt a little bit 'Partridge-by-numbers'. We
were also keen to avoid slipping into spoof territory – it would have felt
too 'knowing'. It's the same reason we rejected names for the film that
sounded like they were sending up a genre: Chap of Steel, Day of the
Partridge, Colossal Velocity. Sorry.

Other drivers must notice him, but he's not embarrassed in the slightest. Why would he be?*

At the musical interlude, he notices a driver on the inside lane and shouts to them.

ALAN
Your fog lamps are on! Your fog lamps are on. There's no fog. There's no fog. No fog!

And he's straight back into the miming, busting out his best moves, until his Bluetooth earpiece falls out.

EXT. RADIO STATION – DAY 2

Alan is getting out of his car. He grabs his laptop bag, shuts the door and locks it — boob beep.

ALAN
Love that noise.

....

* The three of us [Rob, Neil, Steve] talked at length about the best song to use here. Until fairly late in the day we were going to go with a modern track ('Black Heart' by Stooshe), with Alan doing really 'urban' dance moves. Another possibility was 'Thinking of You' by Sister Sledge, but the inevitable air-bass and air-guitar would have made driving hazardous. 'Cuddly Toy' was a better choice, though, and an undeniably great song. The fog lamp bit was another of those that only came up on the day of the shoot, about a minute before we did a take in fact.

FEMALE VOICE
(Off)
Michael, do it outside!

Alan has reached the front door. Security guard
MICHAEL is there, snorting the contents of his
nostrils onto the floor, footballer-style. *

ALAN
Morning, Michael.

MICHAEL
(Saluting)
Morning, Mr Partridge. †

Danny walks past. He holds out a fist for Alan to bump.
Alan puts the flat of his palm over it.

ALAN
Paper.

....

* Comedy doesn't get more unsophisticated than Michael snotting up
on the ground. We tried to add a little extra to it in post-production
with the voice of the secretary. A few of us might – if it were some sort
of nasal emergency – clear our nose like this, but only Michael would try
to do it inside and have to be told to leave the building. The man's little
better than a wild animal.

† This scene originally featured an exchange in which Alan and
Michael bemoan the fact that Michael can't restrain mouthy teenagers if
they're not on company property. We removed it in the end – what with
suntanned children and Bobby Brushes in the first 10 minutes, it felt as
if we had a vendetta against kids.

DANNY
I was doing a fist bump.

ALAN
Yes, well, you would say that, now you've lost.

DANNY
No, it's instead of a handshake.

ALAN
(Shouting after him)
Yes, some people say it's more hygienic than a
handshake, but who's to say you can't get shit on
your fist?

Danny gets in his car.

MICHAEL
Hey, did you hear him making fun of you earlier?

ALAN
I did, Michael, but as Oscar Wilde said, 'There's
only one thing worse than being talked about …'

MICHAEL
Cancer.

ALAN
No, not being talked about.

MICHAEL
(Sickened)
What, Oscar Wilde said not being talked about was
worse than cancer?

ALAN
Yes, yes. I think he was at a party. Probably just
being a gay show-off.

INT. RADIO STATION – RECEPTION/CORRIDOR – DAY 2

Alan heads into reception, laptop bag over shoulder.

*Behind the reception desk, workmen are up a ladder
putting up a new sign: 'Shape – the way you want it to
be'. On the ground lies the old sign: 'North Norfolk
Digital'.*

As Alan looks at the new sign, he hears Dave on-air.

DAVE
Do you know what I really like? I like waking up in
the morning, breathing in the air, and actually
realising I've made it through the night and I
haven't wet the bed! No, I am joking, obviously,
but they were, of course, very, very dark days
indeed.

(Brightly)
But they're all behind me now!*

He's now walking alongside receptionist ANGELA (40).

ALAN
Morning, Angela.

ANGELA
Morning, Alan.

ALAN
Walking and talking, like *The West Wing*.
'Mr President, we have a code red!'

ANGELA
(Cutting in)
I've never seen the show.

ALAN
No, me neither. Corner coming up.

ANGELA
You never know what's around the corner.

....

* We'd figured out early in the writing process that Dave Clifton was the returning character we wanted to give a twist to. He's now put his drinking days behind him and rather than annoying Alan by directly confronting him, he now does it completely obliviously via being too cheery and too open about his troubled past. We had a very clear idea of how we wanted Phil Cornwell to say these lines. As always, his delivery was superb.

ALAN
More corners, usually.

She stops at a door. He's keen to keep the conversation going.

ALAN (CONT'D)
Imagine a world without corners.

ANGELA
(Confidently)
Then we won't be able to cut any. Everybody would be going round in circles.

On that, she walks through the door and shuts it behind her. It's the disabled toilet.

ALAN
Wow!

He dwells on the exchange for a second.

ALAN (CONT'D)
I enjoyed that.

INT. RADIO STATION – STAFF AREA – DAY 2

Alan walks back to the staff area and we hear Dave through the speakers.

DAVE
(On-air)
Actually, I will tell you one thing. It did strike me that, when I was going through my bad times, I found Norfolk was perhaps maybe not the place to be … just because it's so flat. There was a sort of bleakness about the place …

As Alan hangs up his jacket, Pat appears.

PAT
You're a good broadcaster, Alan, don't forget that.*

ALAN
I wasn't planning to, Pat.

PAT
Have you seen this memo? Exciting new phase. Here's to the future. My days are numbered, mate.

....

* On the day this scene was shot, the caterers made sticky toffee pudding. Very nice.

ALAN
Pat, no one's getting sacked; it's just a rumour.
It's like Bobby Brushes the caretaker when the
swimming pool allegations came out.

PAT
He was in bits.

ALAN
Yes, and in the end he was just helping those lads
towel off. He was being nice. He didn't even know
them.

PAT
Yes, but where is he now?

ANGELA
Runs his own business.

ALAN
There, you see, he's back on his feet.

ANGELA
Rents out bouncy castles.

ALAN
(Suddenly concerned)
For adults, yeah?

PAT
I don't know, Alan. Look at this memo.

ALAN

I've seen the memo. It's quite simple; Gordale
Media are simply reimagining our core brand values
and giving us a name more fitting to multi-platform
content delivery. They're people people.

PAT

People people sack people.

ALAN

No, Pat. People sack people. People people please
people, you know that.

ANGELA

Can you have a word with them, Alan?

PAT

Would you?

ALAN

Sure, I mean yes, as soon as I can get them all in
the same room together, which is not an easy tas—

ANGELA

Well, they're all up in the boardroom.

ALAN

Well, that's great.

PAT

Thank you, thank you, Alan. You're a pal.

ALAN (CONT'D)
Well, pals is pals.

INT. RADIO STATION - MEETING ROOM - DAY 2

*Jason, Greg and about eight metropolitan-looking
executives are at a boardroom table. They don't look
like 'Alan' people. Feels like an important meeting.*

JASON
So, if we're all looking at the last quarterly
figures for North Norfolk on page six, and then if
you turn to page five …

Alan knocks and pokes his head round the door.

ALAN
Hi, guys! Don't want to be an agenda bender, but
any chance of a quick 'wa-wa'?

GREG
It's actually not a good time, Alan.

JASON
No, no, it's fine. We've got time. Come in.

GREG
Oh, yes, because we moved the other thing, didn't
we, to free up this. Yes, it's a good time.

Alan extends his hand to Jason.

ALAN
Alan, Alan Partridge.

JASON
Jason Tresswell, MD of Gordale Media.

ALAN
Right. By the way, it's not Alan Alan Partridge,
it's Alan comma Alan Partridge. I know some people
do have two names together.

JASON
Yes, Zsa Zsa Gabor, for instance.

ALAN
Ha!

GREG
Yes! And Duran Duran. They'd have something to say
about that!

ALAN
Yeah, not as good. Er … Kris Kris Tofferson?
Excellent small talk. Gentlemen, to business!

He stands at the head of the table.

ALAN (CONT'D)
Okay, I am here as one of the more senior D-Jocks
at this station. I'm going to talk about jobs.

He's removing his gloves finger by finger.

ALAN (CONT'D)
Like a Nazi officer this, isn't it? I should snap
my heels together.
(German accent)
Achtung!

EXEC
(Joining in)
Guten Tag!

ALAN
Silence!

*He slaps him with his glove.**

ALAN (CONT'D)
Sorry, I meant to miss you! Okay, I want you to do
something for me. I want you to take all your
prejudices, put them in a box marked 'Prejudices',
put them to one side, wipe the prejudice juice off
your hands …

*As he talks, Alan glances at the chart on the desk. It
has a list of DJs on it, and Pat's name is circled in
red marker.*

....

* We came up with this whole Nazi thing, and the bit at the end with
the gloves, in between takes. We had a couple of minutes to play with
and felt the scene needed a couple of bigger gags. If in doubt, go with
the Nazis.

JASON
Alan, could I just stop you there? Change is
healthy, you shouldn't fear it.

ALAN
I'm not scared of anything, not even an elephant,
which is interesting, because there's one in this
room. Want to know his name?

EXEC 2
Pat Farrell?

ALAN
It's Pat Farrell. Pat's audience is old. Old
people, much like dogs, are blindly loyal, and if
Pat hightails it to Cedar FM and they follow,
you've got a grey exodus on your hands. A grexodus.

He lets that sink in.

ALAN (CONT'D)
Hmmm, that prejudices box, it doesn't seem quite so
cool anymore, does it?

EXEC
Yes, but we bought Cedar FM as well.

ALAN
I didn't know that. I did not know that. The point
is …

*Alan looks down again. Further down the list is his
name, also circled in red. His mouth goes dry.*

JASON
You were talking about Pat Farrell.

ALAN
Thanks. Pat Farrell is a great guy. He's always the
first to speak up at union meetings, you know,
being a member of a union.

Someone makes a note of this.

ALAN (CONT'D)
I don't know if you know, but he's also Irish,
which is, weirdly, a plus point — if you like
swearing. He's often on his show, saying fecking
this and fecking that. I know that some Irish
people say that 'feck off' isn't as bad as 'fuck
off', but I think that's bullshit, or 'bellshit'.
Bottom line is, he swears too much.

JASON
This is all very interesting, Alan, but …

ALAN
Okay, I can sum up Pat Farrell in 10 words. 'Pat
isn't very good so let him go … guys … seriously.'
I can condense that to three words.

*He takes a marker pen and scrawls the three words on
the flipchart as he says them:*

ALAN (CONT'D)
Just sack Pat.
The man's a burden. I can help Shape. If I thought
I was a burden, I'd fire myself. I'd kill myself.

JASON
Go on then, how?

ALAN
Run into the sea after a big meal?

JASON
No, I meant, how would you help Shape?

ALAN
I'll show you. Got loads of ideas. Starting with
the Shape of Shape, a social media platform that —
both uniquely and somehow — tracks the location of
all our listeners in real time. Wanna know more? I
do.

*He takes his laptop from his bag and plonks it on the
desk. He opens the laptop. He waits. The screen
suddenly comes to life and we see the web page he was
last on, titled 'Big Pecs NOW!!' next to a bottle of
pills.*

He clicks it shut. It crashes.

ALAN (CONT'D)
That's just a bench-press thing.

GREG
Alan, we're sort of in the middle of something
here.

ALAN
It's fine, jus' need to start up the CD. When this
happens usually, I make a joke that it's a
PowerPoint Presentation. I've got a PPP, sounds
like I'm desperate for the loo. I won't do that
joke …

JASON
Alan, why don't you just leave me the CD?

*Alan presses the eject button but can't get the DVD
tray to open. He fiddles for ages.*

ALAN
Good idea. It should come out … Normally, it waits
a second, then … No, it's not going to do it. Okay!

*He marches over to the buffet and starts to prise the
DVD tray open with a knife.*

JASON
Alan, no, come on …

ALAN
No, no, no, no! It's fine.

No joy. He picks up the laptop …

ALAN (CONT'D)
Just give myself a head start.

... *and slams it onto the floor.*

He ends up snapping the screen off the keyboard and then pulling the keyboard apart until the tray comes out.* Keys and other bits fall off onto the floor. He hands the CD over.

ALAN (CONT'D)
There you go. I'm a finisher, I'll say that for myself. Chill out!

Out of breath, he pats Jason on the shoulder.

ALAN (CONT'D)
That completes my presentation. Gentlemen, I'll leave you to your biscuits.

....

* Smashing up his laptop felt like Alan was acting too mad, too early. Originally, the film had opened with Alan at the BBC, having been invited to pitch some ideas. He wrongly assumed it was a one-on-one meeting. It was actually more like an open day where producers could come and talk through their ideas publicly. So Alan was surrounded by young, trendy TV producers, giving slick multi-media presentations. When his computer stalled and he couldn't get the disc out he ended up breaking it open so he could hand it to the BBC execs. In that version of the scene it's easier to see why Alan would go to those lengths. It didn't work as well when we tried to reuse it in this boardroom scene. And from a logical point of view, if Alan had acted this weirdly in the boardroom, he'd have been the one sacked, not Pat.

*He leaves, accidentally dropping his gloves on the way
out. After a second, his hand reaches back in for
them.*

    ALAN (CONT'D)
    (Off)
    Gloves.

But he only manages to take one. Another pause.

    ALAN (CONT'D)
    (Off, whispered)
    Oh, fuck.

His hand reaches in.

    ALAN (CONT'D)
    (Off)
    Glove.

This time he gets it.

INT. RADIO STATION – STUDIO – DAY 2

*Alan on-air with Simon. He takes a swig of tea and
swallows loudly.*

    ALAN
    Ah! That was soft-rock cocaine enthusiasts
    Fleetwood Mac, and this was Mid Morning Matters
    where, once again, mid morning …

SIMON
Mattered.

ALAN
… mattered.

Simon was slightly out on his timing and knows it straight away. Over a jingle, Alan lays into him.

ALAN (CONT'D)
You're supposed to do it in sync, right. Always leave a gap after the first words.

SIMON
That's right, I'm sorry.

ALAN
Simple, very simple.

The jingle ends, and through the glass Alan sees Pat — almost trancelike — approaching. He looks shell-shocked and has put his belongings into a box.

Alan looks away quickly to the wall, which is now covered in laminates bearing a Shape logo on them and slogans like 'BE RELEVANT', 'TALK WITH A SMILE', 'LIVE THE BRAND', 'LOCAL LOCAL LOCAL' and 'SHAPE — THE WAY YOU WANT IT TO BE'. Right in his eyeline is a laminated instruction: REPEAT THE NAME. Alan closes his eyes.

ALAN (CONT'D)
You're listening to … Shape.

*Alan sees that below the laminate is another that
says: AND THE STRAPLINE.*

> ALAN (CONT'D)
> The way you want it to be.

*As he fades a song up and removes his cans, Pat is
almost at the door with his box of belongings,
including the protruding feet of some green cuddly
toy.*

Alan grabs his phone.

> ALAN (CONT'D)
> (On the phone)
> Mm-mm. Right, and will it take long? It <u>will</u> take
> long, okay.
> (To Pat)
> Hi, Pat, I'll catch you later.
> (On phone)
> Well, I'm not happy about it, but I'll just …

*The mobile rings. Alan nudges it off slyly and carries
on.*

> ALAN (CONT'D)
> (On phone)
> … just have to go along with it, won't I? The
> problem is that the phone rings even when I'm
> speaking on it, so it sounds bloody weird! In fact,
> it just did it then. Did you hear it?
> (Re the caller)
> Yes, he heard it.

(On phone)
Okay, well, I'll leave it with you. Mm-mm, yes.
Yes. Alright. Thanks, Susan.

He winces at his error as he hangs up.

ALAN (CONT'D)
If Geoff Susan doesn't mend that phone there'll be
hell to pay.

PAT
They wouldn't even let me say goodbye to my
listeners. Just gave me 30 minutes to clear out my
locker.

ALAN
At least I'm getting their mugs dirty.

PAT
Thanks, Alan. You always stuck up for me, not like
the others. Well, I'll let you get back to Geoff.

He leaves.

ALAN
(To Simon)
Who's Geoff?

SIMON
Geoff Susan.

ALAN
Oh, yes, of course.

INT. ALAN'S BEDROOM EN-SUITE/BEDROOM – NIGHT
2

Alan is dressed in party gear, trimming his nose hair painfully. Lynn swipes her finger across a brand-new iPad.

ALAN
I did the right thing, didn't I, Lynn? I mean, I think he knew his days were numbered. It was more of an assisted suicide, really. I just flew him to Switzerland, filled out a few forms and sloped off to the airport.

He stops and looks at her.

ALAN (CONT'D)
I've got to be honest, Lynn, I'm feeling pretty crummy.

LYNN
Pat's Irish, isn't he?

ALAN
To be sure.

LYNN
Why don't you donate £50 to Sinn Féin?

ALAN
Perfect!

EXT. RADIO STATION - NIGHT 2

The Shape branding is plastered all over the building.

Alan and Lynn get out of his car and walk to the entrance. He locks the car. Boop Beep.

ALAN
Love that noise. Just keep me away from the sausage rolls. I've started wearing my chubby clothes again.

LYNN
I noticed.

ALAN
What, the chub or the clothes?

Lynn laughs and hands him his iPad.

LYNN
iPad.

ALAN
My pad.

Lynn laughs even louder.

ALAN (CONT'D)
It's not that funny, Lynn.

39

INT. RADIO STATION – RECEPTION/PARTY ROOM – NIGHT 2

Montage of the party in full swing. We hear a few snippets of conversation, maybe mixed up with shots of people laughing, the new branding, mojitos, trendy canapés, etc. It feels young and vibrant, unlike NND. Dave is talking to Simon. We just see chopped-up chunks of his dialogue.

> DAVE
> I used to go with prostitutes.

> SIMON
> Brilliant.

> DAVE
> Cocaine, that was the trigger. You know: cocaine, prostitutes. Bit of a cycle. Puking up the old luminous green bile.
> (Laughing)
> I was withdrawing!

EXT. RADIO STATION – NIGHT 2

Alan enters with Lynn. He has an iPad with him. Three or four women in Shape T-shirts hand out mojitos. Michael follows them in.

> LYNN
> I'm sure they'll have a proper spread. Finger food and the like.

ALAN
Lynn, this ain't sausage rolls down the church
disco. It's canapés, hors d'oeuvres, amuse-bouches.

LYNN
Amuse-bouches?

ALAN
It's literally 'French mouth amusement'.

LYNN
(Shocked)
Oh.

In the studio we see that Wally Banter is on-air.

WAITRESS
Welcome to Shape.

ALAN
Who are you?

Michael nudges him.

MICHAEL
I see they've taken down your photo.

*The mugshots have all been replaced by a blibby
abstract painting. Alan frowns.*

ALAN
They've taken them all down.

41

LYNN
Perhaps they're cleaning them.

MICHAEL
Why have they put that up?

ALAN
I don't know.

LYNN
It's very colourful, very upbeat.

ALAN
It looks like a clown's shot himself in the head.

MICHAEL
Aye! 'All you kids stop laughing at me!'

He mimes shooting himself in the mouth.

MICHAEL (CONT'D)
'Ahhh, the clown's dead!!'

The girl handing out drinks looks concerned. *

....

* Always nice to see Michael, and good to see the three of them together. Useful symbolism, too – the new, vague picture replacing the old mugshots. Something personal, if old-fashioned, replaced by something modern but generic. Not very funny, though.

ALAN
(To girl)
Don't mind Michael, he's got, er, p—

MICHAEL
Post-traumatic stress disorder.

ALAN
(To himself)
I was going to say a penchant for mime.*

Alan and Lynn stand to one side.

LYNN
Okay, how are you feeling?

ALAN
I feel a bit nervous, Lynn. I've got gas again and
I've only just got rid of a nasal whistle.

He attempts a sip of his drink but nothing comes up.

ALAN (CONT'D)
It's a stirrer, not a straw.

....

* The dialogue was solid enough but it had to go for length. We shot
almost three hours of stuff overall, but we wanted the film to be no
longer than 90 minutes, so lots had to be culled.

LYNN
Why don't you do what you did before your advanced
driving test? When you were a bag of nerves?
Pretend to be Roger Moore.

ALAN
Lynn, that never works …

LYNN
Try it.

Angela walks by and he walks along with her.

ANGELA
Hello, Alan.

ALAN
(Roger Moore voice)
Ah, hello, Angela.

ANGELA
Have you got a cold?

ALAN
(To Lynn)
See!

ALAN
I've got my minder with me.

ANGELA
Lynn?

44

ALAN
Yes. She might not seem tough, but I once saw her
stamp on 50 cockroaches in a minute.

LYNN
He didn't see. He was in the next room. It was in
Wales.

ALAN
That's true, yes. All I could hear was crunch,
crunch, crunch, stamp, stamp, stamp. I thought she
was country dancing whilst eating cereal.

LYNN
I thought it was the end of days. They were legion.

ALAN
Lynn likes the Bible.

ANGELA
I've never understood moths. They only come out at
night, yet they're attracted to the light. I don't
know why they just don't come out during the day.

ALAN
I've nothing to add to that. In fact, if you
substituted butterflies …
(To Lynn)
Sorry, can you get me some sausage rolls?
(To Angela)

If you substituted butterfly for moth, I think it
would sound like poetry. Yes, unfortunately
Wordsworth didn't say, 'I wandered lonely as a
moth, to eat some jumpers in a drawer.'

ANGELA
(Joining in)
'As if that wasn't bad enough, it ate my sock upon
the moor.'

Pause.

ALAN
Yes. It's just why a sock would be on the moor. A
mitten, maybe.

INT. RADIO STATION – RECEPTION/PARTY ROOM – NIGHT 2

DAVE
And I actually spewed up some of my stomach lining.
I don't know if you've ever done any horse, have
you?

SIMON
I've ridden a donkey.

DAVE
No, no, no, I mean heroin.

SIMON
I know what you mean. No, I've not done heroin.

INT. RADIO STATION – RECEPTION/PARTY ROOM – NIGHT 2

Jason is holding court, talking to Greg and Danny.

JASON
I don't like subtitles in my films. *Citizen Kane*, black and white, haven't seen that. Tell you what, the best film for me, ever, is still *The Godfather*.

DANNY
Amazing film. 'I'm going to make him an offer he can't refuse.' Amazing acting!

Alan sidles up.

ALAN
Great acting. I tell you what's even better. A lot of people are shocked when I say this: the camera angles.*

LYNN
Alan, I need a word.

JASON
Camera angles?

Lynn drags him to one side.

....

* Felicity Montagu (she plays Lynn) always liked this line. A good woman.

47

LYNN

It's rather delicate. Remember when you took me for that Christmas meal at the ice rink?

ALAN

Of course I do, Lynn. You insisted we sit near the skaters and those boys kept skidding ice at me.

LYNN

You remember that woman disinfecting the boots, the one that took a shine to you? I went home, and you and her … well, it's none of my business.

ALAN

It is none of your business, Lynn, but yes, for the record, went back to her place. Yes, watched *Air Crash Investigation*, then I fell asleep in her big armchair. Perfectly normal woman.

LYNN

Well, she's here.

In the back of shot, BERNIE, a 45-year-old Welsh woman, is necking a glass of champagne and getting stuck into another one.

ALAN

(Panicked)

Lynn, get rid of her! She's a drunk racist. I'll tolerate one, but not both.

EXT. RADIO STATION – NIGHT 2

Alan is leading Bernie from the building. Lynn follows a few yards behind, but Alan's aware she might be able to hear.

Meanwhile, a blurred figure gets out of a car parked behind Alan and gets something from the boot. *

BERNIE
But you said I could pop by any time.

ALAN
I know, but my career's hanging by a thread in there.

BERNIE
And I'm an embarrassment, am I?

ALAN
No, no.

BERNIE
You just wanted sex. You used me.

....

* This was another of the scenes we shot twice. We ditched the smashing up the laptop stuff (see footnote on page 33), which had a few knock-on effects, one being that we needed to redo Bernie's exit. We also wanted to have another go at seeing Pat enter the building with his rifle, unseen by Alan. Declan Lowney (our director) did a brilliant job of only letting the viewer glimpse a shadowy figure passing across the back of the shot.

ALAN
Well, maybe you used me. I didn't have much of a
say over what went on that night.

BERNIE
I didn't hear you complaining.

ALAN
(Quiet)
I couldn't speak.

BERNIE
See you around mine again, then.

ALAN
I don't know …

BERNIE
What's wrong with my place?

ALAN
Well, all those dogs barking.

BERNIE
But it's their bedroom, too.

By now, Lynn's had enough and takes Bernie by the arm.

LYNN
Bernie, may I have a word?

*She leads her to the taxi. Alan watches, but can't
make out what Lynn's saying.*

BERNIE
(Quiet)
He's talking clap ... crap. Listen to me. I sound
like a Chinky. I can't fucking speak when I'm
pissed ...

Behind him, out of focus, the blurred figure holding
something gun-like walks into the building. Two
gunshots light up the window.

Alan is about to turn and look when he hears ...

LYNN
There we go. All done.

Lynn's back. Bernie is being driven away.

ALAN
What did you say to her?

LYNN
I told her that God loves everyone. Even sluts.

ALAN
Goodnight, Lynn.

LYNN
Night, Alan.

INT. RADIO STATION - PARTY ROOM - NIGHT 2

Alan goes back into the party, desperately trying to gee himself up so he can make a good impression. He doesn't notice the spilt drinks and trays of food strewn on the floor.

As he walks down the corridor, he gets into the beat of the music, rolls his jacket sleeves up to look cool, then thinks better of it and rolls them back down.

He re-enters the main room to find there's no one there. It's like a ghost town. The fire exit is open, a single woman's shoe is on the floor and some drinks are on the floor, recently spilled.

ALAN
Hello? V. funny, tee-hee. Very impressive. 'Oh, they must have left in a hurry. Something weird's happened.'

Behind him, through the soundproofed glass, Sidekick Simon is thrown across the room. Alan heads back the way he came.

ALAN (CONT'D)
All right, you've freaked me out. So just, if I could …

He sees something through the porthole window of the studio.

ALAN (CONT'D)
There you are! Pat?

He ducks away from the window as a gunshot blast shatters the glass.

Alan flees.

Halfway down a corridor, he trips over himself and takes a tumble.

ALAN (CONT'D)
I'm down!

He gets up and runs for his life. He can hear Pat's footsteps behind him. He hides around a corner and as the footsteps reach him he picks up a fire extinguisher.

He tries to read the instructions, then has a better idea. Wallop. He slams it into the onrushing Pat. Except it's not Pat, it's Simon. Now he's groaning on the floor.

ALAN (CONT'D)
You step to me?!

He sees who it is.

ALAN (CONT'D)
Simon! Yes, all right, I'll go on without you.

He takes the extinguisher and places it into Simon's hand, like a murderer might do with a gun to make it look like suicide, before realising that it makes far less sense with a fire extinguisher. He runs.

EXT. RADIO STATION - NIGHT 2

Alan hurtles out of the door, across the car park and past the camera. He's shitting himself.

CUT TO:

EXT. STREET/POLICE STATION - NIGHT 2

We see all this action from maybe 40 feet away.

Alan is legging it down the street, next to Norwich City Hall. A car approaches. In his panic, Alan tries to stop it by thumbing a lift, then steps into the middle of the road and raises his hands. The car stops.

ALAN
I need to commandeer this vehicle.

WOMAN
What?*

ALAN
There's a madman with a gun.

No response.

ALAN (CONT'D)
He's Irish!

WOMAN
Get in.

He gets in the driver's side and the car speeds off.

ALAN
Why do you sit so close to the wheel? I could steer
with my balls.† Where's the nearest police station?

WOMAN
Just here.

....

* The woman driving this car was actually a stuntman dressed as an old woman, complete with make-up and handbag. Given how much effort was spent on that costume it's nice to think that when you watch the scene you're nowhere near close enough to make out who's driving. Still, he seemed to enjoy it.

† All of this was invented as we were about to do a take. Steve wanted Alan to comment on the woman's seating position and Neil chipped in with the 'balls' line. Declan, our director, suggested the 'Just here' bit. I drank a coffee.

*He slams on the brakes. They've travelled maybe 20
yards.*

ALAN
Oh! Thanks.

WOMAN
Are you Alan Partr—?

He slams the car door shut and leaps up the steps.

INT. POLICE STATION FRONT DESK – NIGHT 2

Alan is mid-chat with a uniformed policewoman.

ALAN
Assault, battery, kidnap, chronic thuggery,
brandishment, actual bodily harm, grievous bodily
harm, harm …

POLICEWOMAN
Just stick to what you saw and we'll decide if it's
ABH or GBH.
(Pronounced as 'haitch')

ALAN
You mean 'aitch'?*

....

* This is one of Steve's own bugbears, so we decided to give it to Alan.
Where does Steve end and Alan begin? You decide.

POLICEWOMAN
That's what I said.

ALAN
Nearly. You said 'haitch'. 'H' is the sound of the
letter, aitch is its name. One is 'h', the other is
aitch. Neither is haitch. Sorry, I'm a bit nervous.

SARGE appears behind him.

SARGE
Mr Partridge. There's something else we need to
talk to you about.

ALAN
(Scared)
Oh!

SARGE
You're not in trouble.

ALAN
(Brightly)
Oh, fine.

EXT. RADIO STATION/INT. SCHOOL/POLICE
INCIDENT ROOM - NIGHT 2

A hive of activity around the radio station. Police cars, officers cordoning off the station, an electricity generator being set up. A police car pulls up. Alan and an officer get out. The officer leads Alan into the school next to the radio station. It has been commandeered by the police for use as a makeshift incident room.

Alan stops and looks back at the buzz of activity. He looks like a kid in a sweet shop.

ALAN
I've never been in a police car before. May I lower the window, please?

The car stops and Alan is shown out. He extends his hand when he sees Sarge.

ALAN (CONT'D)
Officer. You were at the police station.

SARGE
Yes, I was just in the car with you. Follow me, please.

He leads the way. Alan looks back again at the flashing lights and drinks it in.

SARGE (CONT'D)
This way, please, sir.

ALAN
Yes. Let's do it.

Alan does a cool Skywalker jog into the building.

INT. SCHOOL/POLICE INCIDENT ROOM - NIGHT 2

Sarge leads Alan through the building. He goes past a room where we see a number of Shape partygoers giving their statements. Then he's into the main incident room. Acting Chief Constable JANET WHITEHEAD is there to greet him. Other cops buzz around in the background.

SARGE
Mr Partridge, this is the Gold Commander of the operation.*

Alan laughs. No one else does.

ALAN
Seriously, is that what you're called?

....

* This scene and the following one were in the script from an early stage. Seeing Alan trying to impress people he sees as senior to him and also being given an opportunity to show off his knowledge of firearms and counter-terrorism techniques always felt like things that had to be in there. It's the tug-of-war between natural cowardice and his arousal at being part of a police incident.

JANET
On this operation, yes. I'm Acting Chief Constable
Janet Whitehead.

Alan bows his head slightly.

ALAN
An honour.

*A smartly dressed man at a desk, MARTIN FITCH, pipes
up without turning round.*

MARTIN
And I'm Martin Fitch. Send.

*He hits return and then stands up.**

MARTIN (CONT'D)
From Scotland Yard's Hostage and Crisis unit, here
to lead the negotiation.

ALAN
A little bit awkward. Who's in charge?

....

* Martin was originally written as quite the cool maverick. We
imagined him and Janet as two senior officers getting aroused by the
tension of the situation and enjoying the feeling of being in their own
TV-like drama. Similarly, Don (who appears in the next scene) was
much more of a clown in earlier drafts. It could have worked, but in the
context of the whole film we had to ration how much comedy derived
from the police. Too much, and the jeopardy collapses.

MARTIN
Make no mistake, this lady is in charge. So here's
the situation. Pat is refusing to speak to us
directly. He's willing to give us three hostages,
but only if he can talk to us through you.

JANET
Now we need to know why Pat has done this, so we
can draw things to a peaceful conclusion.

ALAN
Yes, sure, I'll talk to him. Deal.

He goes to shake Martin's hand.

ALAN (CONT'D)
Sorry, wrong person. Come here.

He kisses her on both cheeks. Awkward pause.

MARTIN
Okay. Now, are you on any medication?

ALAN
Just some cream. I've got very aggressive athlete's
foot, but that's the only thing about me that is.

MARTIN
And do you suffer from any nervous conditions, such
as panic attacks?

ALAN
(Snorting)
Do I look like I suffer from panic attacks? I've
had one panic attack, in a car wash. It was a
perfect storm of no sleep, no wife and angry
brushes whirring towards me. By the time the giant
hairdryer came on I was in the footwell.

MARTIN
Does the idea of weaponry trouble you?

ALAN
No, no. I've fired several rifles … at funfairs,
and won prizes. But I've never fired one in anger.
Or at a cat.

JANET
We'll have you fully briefed by the Tactical
Firearms team …

ALAN
Cool.

JANET
… and we'll be keeping in regular phone contact
with you when you go in.

ALAN
Very cool. Sorry, 'go in'? What, into the building?

JANET
Mm-mm.

ALAN
To speak to Pat in person?

JANET
Yes, is that not what you …?

MARTIN
Everything okay?

ALAN
Yes. I'm just a little nervous about going into a
car wash, er … siege.

MARTIN
So, what do you say, Al? Will you help us?

Alan sighs and sits down. All eyes are on him.

ALAN
(Milking it)
Guys, none of us choose the hand we're dealt. But
y'know, it's funny …

JANET
We do need an answer, I'm afraid.

ALAN
Why, have you got another siege to go to? It was my
understanding that if you say yes to something like
this, you get to say a few words.

MARTIN
So you are saying yes?

ALAN
Well, yes, but I was going to leave that bit to the
end.

MARTIN
Good man, okay.

SARGE
If you'd like to come with me.

*The police disperse. Alan is led away and sees that a
police camcorder has been taping them.*

ALAN
Can I have a copy of that?

INT. SCHOOL/POLICE FIREARMS ROOM – NIGHT 2

*Alan is being briefed by STEVE STUBBS. Someone is
fitting his bullet-proof vest. Other armed officers are
buzzing around.*

STEVE STUBBS
Right, sir, let's keep this simple, shall we?

ALAN
Roger that.

STEVE STUBBS
No heroics.

ALAN
Ten four, good buddy.

STEVE STUBBS
Do not physically engage him.

ALAN
But it's fight a gun, flee a knife, yes?

STEVE STUBBS
And where did you read that?

ALAN
I've got to say, big fan of you guys in TFU. If I had my way, all police officers would carry firearms.

STEVE STUBBS
I personally think that firearms should remain in the hands of the specialists.

ALAN
Me too. What I was going to go on to say was that all police officers should carry guns, but only specialists should be allowed to fire them. And if you think I've just made that point of view up, call my assistant and she'll …

STEVE STUBBS
(Snapping)
Alan! Read my lips. Now, if you jeopardise the
safety of any of my men or any of those hostages
inside that building because you've not been
listening to me, I will take off this police
uniform and I will make you pay for it.

ALAN
You want me to buy your police uniform off you?

STEVE STUBBS
No, but I'll give you a fucking good hiding, is
that clear?

ALAN
Yes. That's clear. Yes, that's clear. You're very
close to me.

STEVE STUBBS
Now, you're a smart bloke, I know you can handle
it. I know you're not going to disappoint me.

ALAN
I won't disappoint you. I aim to please you. And I
hope to impress you.

STEVE STUBBS
Good man.

ALAN
Yes, you're a good man, too.

STEVE STUBBS
Right, well, Don will fill you in.

Steve leaves. By this point the TFU guys in the background have also gone. It's just DON and Alan. Pause.

DON
He has to say all that shit for insurance.

ALAN
Right.

DON
Tell me this much, mate. What's your favourite siege?

ALAN
Iranian embassy.

DON
Same, why?

ALAN
Because they used the sound of a pneumatic drill to disguise the noise of them removing bricks from a neighbouring wall ...

DON
So they could smash through the plaster, and ...

ALAN
... take them out of the game.

BOTH
It's just a great siege.

They enjoy the memory of it.

DON
Hey, do you want to see me gun?

ALAN
Does …
(Can't think of an analogy)
Yes, please. Let's clock the Glock.

DON
(Amused)
You'll have to move quicker than that, there, eh?
Got any last messages for your kids?

ALAN
No, because they don't speak to me anymore!

The laughing stops.

ALAN (CONT'D)
Actually, just ask why don't they speak to me.
Although I wouldn't hear the answer, would I?
Actually, no, just 'I love you'.

Don looks awkward.

EXT. RADIO STATION - NIGHT 2

*Outside the radio station, it's still a hive of
activity. But now there's a sense of tension in the
air. Alan's about to go in. He's carrying a small
bakery bag in one hand and a military-style field phone
in the other. Under his jacket the bullet-proof vest
makes him look awkward and thick-set. He's nervous.*

ALAN
Is this vest made of carbon fibre?

MARTIN
It's made of Kevlar.

ALAN
Oh, yeah, I always get them confused. They're both
high-strength weaves, about five times the strength
of steel.

Martin holds his hand up to say 'halt'.

ALAN (CONT'D)
Kevlar deforms, whereas carbon fibre tends to
shatter.

MARTIN
Shhh!

Martin takes a megaphone.

MARTIN (CONT'D)
Pat! Alan's coming in now!

He motions for Alan to proceed.

    ALAN
    (Earnest)
    Thanks, and I hope I'll be okay.

Alan walks towards the station. He stands in front of the doors, then looks up at the security camera. After a second there's a long beep and the doors open. Alan takes a breath and says to himself:

    ALAN (CONT'D)
    Welcome to big school.*

Martin calls to Pat through a loud hailer.

    MARTIN
    Pat, Alan's coming in now!

Alan walks towards the station. He stands in front of the doors then looks up at the security camera. After a second there's a long beep and the doors open.

INT. RADIO STATION - NIGHT 2

As he enters, the three released hostages scuttle out. One of them is Greg. He sees Alan and looks sheepish.

....

* We ended up cutting this exchange for length, despite the 'big school' line being in the film's trailer. It was more important to inject some pace.

ALAN
(Whispered)
Greg!

GREG
(Whispered)
Oh, hey, Alan. Thanks.

ALAN
(Whispered)
They let you go as well?

GREG
(Whispered)
Oh, yes. I'm just relieved to be getting out of
there.

ALAN
(Whispered)
Aren't there still women in there?

GREG
(Whispered)
Yes, well, I think it'd be a bit sexist to let all
the women go out first.

ALAN
(Whispered)
Yes. Sleep well, Greg.

GREG
Thanks.

INT. RADIO STATION - STUDIO - NIGHT 2

Alan walks nervously down the corridor. He looks in
each studio he passes. They're all empty. Then he
reaches the one with the shot-out window. He moves
closer. He puts his face up to the broken pane and
peers in. He can't see anyone.

    ALAN
    Pat?

He opens the door to the studio gingerly. Suddenly
there's a voice behind him.

    PAT
    Prepare to die!

    ALAN
    Oh, I'm not ready to!

Alan jumps out of his skin and spins round. Pat laughs
and opens the door. He's wearing a spaghetti western
outfit: a poncho (a fire blanket he's cut a hole in), a
belt of cartridges across one shoulder and a leather
belt across the other for symmetry. He's made a
moustache from tape.

PAT
It's okay!
(He removes the moustache)
It's me — Pat. I just thought a little jokey
costume would, you know, put you at ease, give you
a giggle.

ALAN
Mission accomplished.

Pause.

PAT
It's great to see you.

ALAN
Good to see you, too. Actually, I've brought you
some cake, not that you deserve it after that, you
ruddy so-and-so. I should crush it in my hand! Oh,
I already have.* How the devil are you?

PAT
Not bad, not bad.

ALAN
I mean, how are you feeling?

....

* Had to do a few takes of this to make sure the cake 'squidged' up and
through Alan's fingers. The key turned out to be wrapping it in cling
film. Time well spent.

73

PAT
Great.

ALAN
Good.

Alan leaves it. He plonks down the field phone.

ALAN (CONT'D)
Oh, the police told me to bring you this. It's just
a standard field phone, you know, should you feel
the inclination to communicate with the
authorities. Good thing about these things is
they're immune to all the problems and glitches you
get with satellite phones.

Pat has been inspecting it, then smashes it.

ALAN (CONT'D)
But, like I say, it's just an option, really, more
than anything.

PAT
I just realised, when you were asking how I was
feeling, you meant:
(Points to his head)

ALAN
Yes, I did.

PAT
(Holding up the phone)
Does that answer your question?

ALAN
Yes, it does.

Alan glances into the adjoining studio.

ALAN (CONT'D)
Oh, hello, didn't see you there! Someone's been in
the wars.

*We see who he is talking to. On the chair is someone
with their head wrapped in tape, with a socket
fashioned from tape jutting from the side of his
head.* Suddenly, Alan's fear is back.*

PAT
Oh, that's just Simon.

ALAN
Can he breathe through that?

PAT
Of course he can. It's just like wearing a mask.

ALAN
Yes. At least when someone puts you in a mask
you've got a safe word, like 'airbag' or
'crayfish'. What's the hat thing?

....
* Steve had a vision of how he wanted this head holster to look from
very early on in the process. Originally, it was just something he wanted
to do to Tim Key, but we later realised it might be quite a good thing to
use in the film.

PAT
Oh, we made that. It's a head holster.

ALAN
Right, never heard of one of those.

PAT
Yes, I'll show you. Simon? You insert the shotgun,
place on stand and …

*He goes to Simon, takes the tape from his mouth, slots
the gun into the dock and then rests the handle on a
mic stand.*

SIMON
Voilà.

PAT
Hands free. I can move around the studio, do
anything I want and if something happens, I don't
even have to look. Boom, hit the target.

ALAN
Yes. Well, you don't need an accomplice.

PAT
Well, I've got you now.

ALAN
Yes. Thank you.

INT. RADIO STATION - RECEPTION - NIGHT 2

We see Pat's POV. Pat is peeping outside, trying to
see how many cops are out there without being seen
himself. Alan stands by awkwardly. *

ALAN
Pat, I have to ask: is this <u>anything</u> to do with the
IRA?

PAT
What?

ALAN
Yeah, I know. They asked me to ask. I think it's
just because you're Irish with a bee in your
bonnet.

PAT
God, no. I just went home after I was sacked,
looked through my VHS tapes, decided to watch
Beaches, y'know, to get things in perspective, but
just cried my fucking eyes out.

ALAN
Wow ...

....

* We cut this scene because we needed to get going with the siege more
quickly. We did lose something in the process, though. This was the
only time we saw Pat looking outside, checking what the police presence
was like – something a lone hostage taker would definitely do. It also
gave a stronger sense of the chain of events, but you can't have it all.

PAT
Yeah, I know.

ALAN
You've still got a VHS player?

PAT
Oh, and Jason was mean to me. I said, 'Can I at
least say goodbye to my listeners one last time?'
He just ignored me. Didn't even know my name. He
called me Pat Feral. I thought, I'll give you
fucking feral.

ALAN
That's pretty funny.

PAT
And now here I am, with the bloody police
everywhere.

ALAN
All over you like stress-induced eczema.

Checks his hands.

ALAN (CONT'D)
It'll come.*

....

* On the pier at the end, at the point of maximum stress, we had Alan
mentioning stress-induced eczema again, looking down at his hands
and saying, 'It's come.' But we cut the set-up, so we had to cut the
pay-off.

INT. RADIO STATION - STUDIO/HOSTAGE ROOM - NIGHT 2

Pat shows Alan back into the studio. He looks at Alan's vest, with POLICE written on the back.

PAT
So, you're with the police now?

ALAN
Oh, this. No, this is just … I think it's Velcro. Yes, there you go. Feck da police!

He tears off the Velcro police badge.

ALAN (CONT'D)
No, I think they were just worried that if they did take a pot shot at you — it's a siege, you've got a gun — that the bullet might pass through your torso and hit me. Unless, of course, they use dum-dums, which explode inside the body. But no, I said, do not use dum-dums on Pat Feral, Farrell, Feral. I'd rather you used a high-velocity round that passes straight through his body, because he's a personal friend of mine.

PAT
And I suppose if I want to shoot you, I can always aim for the head.

ALAN
Exactly, exactly. I don't even know why I'm wearing it.

PAT
Just take it off.

ALAN
I'll happily take it off.

PAT
Go on.

ALAN
Pat, if you want me to take it off, I'll take it
off.

He doesn't. Pat points the gun at him and shouts.

PAT
Fucking take it off!

ALAN
(Scared)
Oh, Pat, now you're making me want to wear it! You
know, I mean, this is not my bag. I'm a disc
jockey. I'm sorry you got the sack, but I'm 55
years old, I should be at home in bed watching
funny videos on YouTube. Sneezing Panda, or Charlie
Bit My Finger.

Pause.

PAT
Have you seen Fat Woman Falls Down Hole?*

Alan frowns.

HARD CUT TO:

INT. RADIO STATION – STUDIO – NIGHT 2

A few minutes later, they and Simon sit in front of a laptop, laughing. Alan now has his vest off.

ALAN
It's hilarious!

PAT
Yes.

ALAN
Isn't it?

SIMON
Yes. I've seen it before, but yes.

....

* We came up with this whole passage late on the night before we shot it. Like most days, we'd been filming for the best part of 12 hours, then started to look at the scenes for the next day. Long hours, but someone had pinned up a black-and-white photo of Eighties pop beauty Kim Wilde to the wall of our writing room, so it wasn't all bad. The room also contained a chair upholstered in denim, a 'jean sofa'. Nice touches, both.

ALAN
I mean, that should be fenced off, really, but I'm
glad it wasn't.

SIMON
Great.

ALAN
Oh, yes! I'm supposed to ask, where are the
hostages?

PAT
In there.

*He pulls up a blind. The hostages are in the session
studio that connects to the main studio. They stand
up, scared.*

ALAN
Oh, my God! That's like some sort of zoo from
Planet of the Apes. Danny looks a bit bruised.

PAT
I lost my temper, a couple of times.

SIMON
Three times.

PAT
Yes, yes, it was three. Go and say hello. Give them
a slap yourself, if you want.

ALAN
Oh, no, I ...

He thinks about it for a second.

ALAN (CONT'D)
No. I'll just say hello.

INT. RADIO STATION - HOSTAGE ROOM - NIGHT 2

The hostages all look scared.

The door opens. Alan comes in. They all talk over each other.

ANGELA
Alan!

CONNOR
Look, do the police know we're here?

JASON
Alan, what the hell's going on?

ALAN
Hey! Hey, hey, hey, hey, hey! Cool it with the crosstalk. You're supposed to be professional broadcasters.

CONNOR
I'm not, I'm a writer.

ALAN
Now, we're only going to get through this with each
other. Now, I want everyone to shake hands with
everyone else, now, whether you want to or not.

*They all shake hands with each other quietly. Danny
offers his fist and Alan shakes it.*

ALAN (CONT'D)
Paper.

They finish.

ALAN (CONT'D)
Okay, Pat will not communicate directly with the
police, only through me. So, as of now, I am
bullhorn. But I think we're going to be okay.

DANNY
Okay? He hit me.

ALAN
Let's not get into who hit who or who, you know,
may have deserved it.

DANNY
You need to keep him away from me, understand?

ALAN
What I need to do, Danny, in conjunction with
Jason, is crisis management, and I am sure he will
agree there's been plenty of crisis …

JASON
But no management.

ALAN
Cowabunga. Walk with me.

He leads Jason a few paces away and speaks in hushed tones.

JASON
Alan, you do realise you're in the box seat here. You've got the guy's confidence.

ALAN
Yes, I don't know why. I mean, I go for a curry with him once a year, and even then I don't have a starter. Trouble is, he does.

JASON
All I need to know is, can you handle it?

ALAN
Well, put it this way: would you ask that of a man who'd gone paintballing, realised he'd left his goggles at reception but carried on anyway?

JASON
Why?

ALAN
You're looking at him.

They return to the group.

ALAN (CONT'D)
Okay, guys, quick wa-wa. Just had a pow-wow with
Jace. Upshot is, I'm going to be his right-hand man
on this one. He'll be … my left-hand man. The …

He quietly swaps sides with Jason.

JASON
Sorry.

ALAN
The point is, Pat has not gone mad. He has a
grievance, he needs some sort of outlet …

*Suddenly a jingle bursts into life: 'Roll Out the
Farrell, with Pat Farrell on North Norfolk Digital.'*

PAT
(Brightly)
This is Patrick Farrell, welcoming you to Roll Out
the Farrell on North Norfolk Digital!

Alan turns back to the group.

ALAN
Okay, Pat may have gone mad. He may have gone mad.

INT. SCHOOL/POLICE INCIDENT ROOM – NIGHT 2

Silence. Close-up of a radio being carried into the room by a WPC. Pat is broadcasting.

PAT
(On radio)
And now we have a text from Cynthia, in Holt, who writes, 'Dear Pat, we are sending you a bottle of our …'

The WPC approaches Janet with the radio.

WPC
Ma'am, I think you'd better listen to this.

PAT
(On radio)
… homemade plum brandy. We use it to make brandy butter, which we …

JANET
Why am I listening to shit radio?

WPC
That's Pat Farrell, ma'am. He's broadcasting from the siege.

PAT
(On radio)
Mm, yum, Cynthia, can't wait.

ALAN PARTRIDGE: ALPHA PAPA

INT. SCHOOL/POLICE INCIDENT ROOM/RADIO STATION – STUDIO – NIGHT 2

Martin and Janet chat to Alan. He's on speakerphone.

Intercut with Alan in the studio, speaking to them while sitting across from Pat and Simon, who has had the tape removed from across his mouth.

MARTIN
Can you gently remind Pat that we have an agreement? You are there to communicate with us.

ALAN
Listen, I don't know what it says in your police operations manual or, I don't know, Psychobabble Weekly …

SIMON
(Helping)
The Penguin Book of Sieges?

ALAN
Yes, or the Penguin Book of Sieges, but out here in the field it's plenty different. I got a guy with a gun and a gripe to grind, and he's saying no speaky.

MARTIN
I would really like to establish a dialogue here, Alan. A simple trilateral exchange from Pat to you to me to you to Pat. Do you understand?

88

PAT
(Shouting)
No more interruptions, or else! Do you think I
don't have balls? I've got plenty of balls! I've
got balls coming out of my arse!

ALAN
Did you hear that?

MARTIN
Yes.

ALAN
Well … that's the end of the call. Bye.

INT. RADIO STATION – STUDIO – NIGHT 2

Back in the studio, Pat is on-air.

PAT
You are listening to North Norfolk Digital.

*He presses a sting but it goes, 'Shape – the way you
want it to be'. He grits his teeth and presses another
one, also for Shape. And then a third, which covers
the next few lines.*

PAT (CONT'D)
What's going on? Where are all my jingles?

SIMON
Jason wanted them deleted.

ALAN
Well, he won't have deleted them all.

SIMON
No, he did delete them all.

ALAN
He did delete them all, Pat.

PAT
What?

SIMON
It was jingle genocide.

ALAN
That's not helping, Simon.

PAT
The bastard. Alan, take over from me. I'm going to
straighten him out.

*He grabs the gun from Simon's head holster. The
watching hostages panic. He gets to the door.*

PAT (CONT'D)
Oh, and keep it light.

Pat goes into the hostage room. The jingle ends.

*Left alone, Alan looks for inspiration on the desk.
Behind him, Pat is silently berating Jason. Alan scans
the studio for ideas.*

ALAN
Right. Okay, you're listening to the Pat and Alan
Show, mainly Pat. Tonight's show will be asking …

Alan continues searching for something to say.

ALAN (CONT'D)
… what time does Mike paper slider switch to mouse
his chocolate cups?

SIMON
Doesn't make sense.

ALAN
It doesn't make sense, but if you can rearrange it
to make sense then you can win bins and win
windows. So that's our win-a-bin-and-window-
rearrange-the-sentence-keep-it-light competition.

*Slam! Pat has shoved Jason against the window of the
studio. Jason stares at Alan, his face all squished
up.*

ALAN (CONT'D)
Oh, shit! This is the theme from *Ski Sunday*. Sorry
for swearing.

*He starts the music, gets up and goes out of shot.
Then we see him appear in the hostage room,
desperately remonstrating with Pat as the music plays.*

HARD CUT TO:

INT. RADIO STATION – HOSTAGE ROOM – NIGHT 2

Continuing from the previous scene, Pat opens the door to go back to the studio.

PAT
One hour. And if that jingle isn't word for word what I just said, I am going to shoot you in the feet, then the knees, then the hands, and basically anything you've got two of, like your face.

ALAN
Oh, yes, two-faced.

PAT
One hour.

Pat slams the door behind him.

JASON
One hour. This is impossible. I'm going to fucking die.

CONNOR
What are we going to do?

DAVE
You can't do a top-quality jingle in an hour.

ALAN
(Taking control)
We can do this. Let me tell you a story. Back in
the day, I was MCing a conference for Raynard
Pharmaceuticals. That evening some of the marketing
guys were doing karaoke. I didn't join in. I tended
to shun Japanese culture — this was the
mid-Nineties, it was more acceptable — but high on
a cocktail of champagne and cheap Foster's lager, I
lunged at the microphone. A few minutes later I was
making grown men cry with my rendition of 'Summer
of '69' by Bryan Adams. The thing is, I twisted the
lyrics to 'the summer of '29', invoking memories of
the Wall Street Crash and German hyperinflation.
Remember, many of these guys were in sales …

JASON
(Shouting)
Alan, where are you going with this?

CONNOR
I think the point is he didn't think he was any
good at singing, and it turns out he was quite good
at singing.

ALAN
Yes, that.

ANGELA
And that if you really, really try, you can do
anything.

ALAN
Yes, and that.

JASON
(Shouting)
I don't care! I'm going to fucking die!

ALAN
Hey, hey, I'm trying to save your head, shoulders,
knees and toes.

ANGELA
(Quietly)
Knees and toes.

ALAN
Okay, man up, musos.

DAVE
Well, I used to play synth in a jazz funk band.

ALAN
Great, who else?

CONNOR
I used to be the drummer in Marillion.*

....

* A last-minute line that has the full endorsement of Marillion
themselves. They came to the premiere and everything. Gave out CDs
in the goody bag.

ALAN
Really?

HOSTAGES
You were in Marillion? (Etc.)

ALAN
There's no time for that, but wow, and great.

He puts the bass guitar on.

TONIA
What are you going to do first?

Zoom in on Alan.

ALAN
I'm going to lay down a rhythm track.

EXT. LYNN'S HOUSE – NIGHT 2

Two policemen knock on a dreary suburban front door.
There's the sound of a hundred locks being unbolted.
Then Lynn answers, still in her nightie.

POLICEMAN
Lynn Benfield?

LYNN
I am she.

POLICEMAN
Do you know Mr Alan Partridge?

She knows what this is about.

LYNN
Okay. He wasn't stealing crisps, he just gets
flustered at self-service checkouts and takes
things without scanning them.

POLICEMAN
Miss Benfield …

LYNN
He doesn't like being told to put things in bagging
areas by automated women.

POLICEMAN
No, Miss Benfield, we're here because Mr Partridge
is currently involved in an armed siege. We're
informing you as his next of kin.

*A second while the horror of the siege competes with
the joy of being next of kin. Then she grits her
teeth.*

LYNN
Take me to him.

INT. RADIO STATION – HOSTAGE ROOM/STUDIO – NIGHT 2

A play button is pressed. Alan and the hostages face Pat as he listens to the jingle they've made. While he listens, we glimpse their petrified faces, watching him for his reaction.*

HOSTAGE JINGLE: 'Pat Farrell has a loyal following in the local community, but Gordale Media fucked him over 'cause they don't care about loyalty. The only thing they give a shit about is their profit margins, and if they don't reinstate him he'll take it out on the hostages, even the ones with kids. Better get yourself some body bags!'

Silence.

PAT
   That was beautiful. Could you make me some more?

They hesitate until he points the gun at them.

....

* We actually filmed all the hostages gathered around the microphone recording this jingle, but when we watched it in the edit it felt too silly. We didn't want to lose it altogether, though, so we used reaction shots of the hostages listening (they were just shots we'd taken from elsewhere) and recut the scene so it became them listening to it being played back. Seeing the fear on their faces as they wait for Pat's reaction was much funnier than seeing them singing it.

ALAN
Oh! Er, yes, maybe!

EXT. SCHOOL/POLICE INCIDENT ROOM – NIGHT 2

Establishing shot. We see Lynn arrive at the school in a police car.

INT. SCHOOL/POLICE INCIDENT ROOM/RADIO
STATION – STUDIO – NIGHT 2

Lynn is waiting in the police interview room. In the background, Pat and Alan are on-air.

PAT
(Radio)
Local folk trio Will o' the Wisp won't be coming in now. Apparently, there are road closures in Norwich due to a major police incident.

Sarge enters, turns the radio off and sits down opposite Lynn.

SARGE
Thanks for waiting, Miss Benfield. Now, we're just trying to speak to anyone who can help us build a picture of Pat Farrell, and you said you know him.

LYNN

Well, I made three cakes for him over the last
year, but there was nothing in them that would have
led him to do this. They were very plain.*

SARGE

Yes, that's not one of our lines of investigation.
We'd just like you to tell us what you know about
Pat.

LYNN

Irish, shock of brown curly hair. He's a strong man
with strong arms and a good walk. Moves well.

SARGE
(Politely)
That was very helpful, Lynn.

LYNN

Oh, thank you.

SARGE

Now, how about some coffee?

....

* We ran out of time to do rehearsals before the shoot started, so all our
actors had to come to set and just crack on with it. Plus scenes were
often rewritten the night before, or on the morning, or between takes.
So we were lucky to have a cast that could deliver despite this, a prime
example being Felicity Montagu. As mentioned in the footnote on page
47, good woman.

LYNN
Oh, of course. How do you take it?

SARGE
No, no, we'll get it for you. Just sit there.

Lynn smiles and gets comfy. This makes a nice change.

INT. RADIO STATION – STUDIO/HOSTAGE ROOM – NIGHT 2

Pat is on his feet, pulling the laminated signs off the wall — the ones that remind the DJs what to say and how.

PAT
I hate all this shit, telling us how to speak.

ALAN
They think they're giving us an identity, when they're just …

PAT
… turning us into nobodies. We're just unit shifters for the money men.

ALAN
Sounds quite good.

Pat slumps on the sofa, tired.

PAT
Alan, did you ever imagine what life would be like
in your fifties?

ALAN
I had hopes and dreams. I think we all did.

PAT
Penny for them.

ALAN
Keep the penny, you've got a gun. But yes, I used
to dream that one day I'd drive a brand-new Range
Rover towing a speedboat.

PAT
I used to dream about growing old with someone I
love.

ALAN
Both valid.

PAT
It's not going to happen now, is it? I miss my
Molly so much.

*Pat opens his wallet and takes out a photo. Alan looks
at it.*

ALAN
Who's this chap?

PAT
That's Molly.

ALAN
Yes, of course.

He looks at it for ages.

ALAN (CONT'D)
She's got such … brown hair.

PAT
A year after that was taken, the angels took her.

SIMON
Must have been a few of them.*

Alan glares at Simon.

PAT
Now I've nobody. No wife, no family, no kids.

Alan comes over to the sofa.

ALAN
Got to say, Pat, kids don't make you happy. Some of
the unhappiest times of my life have been with my
kids.

....

* Sidekick Simon's line always got the big laugh in this scene. It was
another of those we wrote the night before. Tim Key's pause before he
delivers the line is what makes it. That's what he says, anyway.

Pat's eyes begin to droop.

ALAN (CONT'D)
I remember a holiday on — on the beach in
Prestatyn. The kids came over to me and said,
'Papa, papa, follow me.' And I followed them about
200 yards across the sand dunes, and when I got
there — finally — all they'd done was dug a big
hole. Miserable.*

PAT
Sounds lovely.

*By now, Pat is almost asleep. Alan looks to Simon, who
nods towards the telephone. Alan looks at it, then
back to Pat. He seems ready to spring into action.*

CUT TO:

INT. RADIO STATION — STUDIO — NEXT MORNING

*Close-up of Alan's face, eyes closed. Then Pat bursts
in.*

PAT
Good morning!

....

* The three of us [Rob, Neil, Steve] were writing this scene a few weeks
before the shoot and this whole passage came out of Steve's mouth fully
formed. He'd just had three Beroccas, which can only have helped.

ALAN
(Mumble)
Crayfish ...

Alan opens his eyes to find Pat is towelling his hair.

PAT
Oh, I feel absolutely great. There's a lot to be
said for a good sleep and a hot shower.

ALAN
Yes.

*Alan looks across to Simon, who has a face like
thunder.*

SIMON
Sleep well, Alan?

ALAN
Yes, thank you.

SKY NEWS REPORT

NEWSCASTER
As the Shape siege enters its first morning, police
are refusing to confirm the number or identities of
the hostages still being held at gunpoint by sacked
DJ Pat Farrell. Fellow DJ Alan Partridge is in
contact with the police, who are now set up at the
school behind me.

INT. RADIO STATION – STUDIO – DAY 3

Pat is broadcasting again — he's taking phone calls from listeners. Simon sits alongside him while Alan sits uselessly on the sofa.

PAT
What would you like us to play, Iris?

IRIS
(On phone)
'Always on My Mind' by Willie Nelson.

PAT
I would love to, Iris, but unfortunately that's not in the system. You see, we're only allowed to play approved tracks.

IRIS
(On phone)
But Pat, you've got a gun, you can play whatever you like.

PAT
Leave it with me and I'll see what I can do, okay?*

....

* This whole scene was a candidate for the cut (it's not funny, the plot would have still worked without it), but it tees up Willie Nelson and plants it in the audience's mind, which is crucial for the climactic scene on the pier.

INT. RADIO STATION - STORE ROOM - DAY 3

Pat and Alan are walking down the corridor to the store room.

PAT
Remember we used to choose our own records?

ALAN
Yes. Or put on a compilation album if you were tired or couldn't be bothered.

They've reached a big walk-in cupboard at the end of the corridor. Pat goes in.

PAT
You like country music, Alan?

ALAN
Can't say I do, Pat. It's just jilted spouses complaining whilst drunk. Also known as a date, if you're over 40.

Alan looks down. Alan stops. Pat's left the gun leaning against the wall. Alan is distracted by it.

PAT
You know, when a listener asks for a song and I don't have it, I feel like I've let them down. Willie Nelson was Molly's favourite, too, and 'Always on My Mind' was her favourite song.

Paralysed by indecision, Alan twitches his fingers.
He's about to take it.

    PAT (CONT'D)
    (Off)
    Do you remember that, the old roadshow bus?

Alan looks up to see Pat beside him with a photo. It's
Pat, Alan and a couple of other DJs in much younger
days, standing in front of a garish yellow broadcast
bus.

    ALAN
    Remember it? I took my family camping in that! That
    was a tough nine days.

    PAT
    You see, this bus brought joy to hundreds.

    ALAN
    I wonder where it is now. Probably impounded after
    it crashed those scouts.

They start to walk back.

    PAT
    No, it's in the basement.

    ALAN
    Oh, I did not know that.

Pat stops.

PAT
Ah, I forgot the record. Hold that, will you?

This time he actually gives the gun to Alan and turns back towards the cupboard. After a step, he stops in his tracks and turns to Alan.

PAT (CONT'D)
Give me the gun, Alan.

Alan looks at it, gripping it tightly.

ALAN
Yeah ...

PAT
The gun, Alan.

ALAN
I was looking at my clothes before. Some people call it gear, don't they? Others call it an outfit. But I call it clobber!

He wallops Pat in the head with the butt of the gun, sending him careering against the wall. The gun goes off, firing into a ceiling tile.

Alan hurtles down a corridor, clutching the gun. The shot has alerted the officers outside, who stream towards the building.

PAT
Alan! Alan! Alan!

Cut to Alan, who has reached reception. Two stun
grenades are thrown through the window and into his
path.

PAT (CONT'D)
Give me the gun, Alan.

Alan panics and hands him the gun.

PAT (CONT'D)
Give me the gun!

MASKED COP 1
Stay where you are! Drop the weapon.
(Gunshot)

Don and another armed cop burst through the doors and
into the reception area. Pat shoots the second cop.

Alan legs it up the stairs and into the meeting room
where he'd earlier scribbled 'Just sack Pat'. He shuts
the door behind him.

PAT
Alan! Alan! Open the door!

ALAN
Just … trying to find some way to escape!

PAT
Alan! Alan!

Before Pat can open the door, Alan hears the sound of
a pneumatic drill, just like the SAS used in the
Iranian embassy siege. It's coming through the far
wall. He thinks for a second, then runs headlong into
the wall …

    ALAN
    Ayyyyyyyatollah!

He bursts through the plaster and ends up in a heap on
the other side.

Alan looks around. Steve Stubbs is sitting in a chair
with headphones on and loads of equipment around him
as if monitoring the raid. But Pat is now through the
door and raising his own weapon.

    ALAN (CONT'D)
    He's got a shooter!

Steve throws off his headphones, grabs a gun off the
back of his chair and fires past Alan at Pat. Pat hits
the ground. Steve turns back to face Alan.

    STEVE STUBBS
    Are you all right, Alan?

    ALAN
    Yes, I'm fine.

But, unseen by Steve, Pat is still alive and reaching
for his gun. Alan sees this.

ALAN (CONT'D)
Cuddle me, cop!

As he's saying this, Alan pulls Steve towards him, as if in a hug, while grabbing the pistol stored in Steve's inside pocket and shooting Pat through Steve's coat. It's superfast and slick. Pat is now dead. Alan takes Steve's radio and speaks into it.

ALAN (CONT'D)
Target down.

Then he hands Steve his pistol as a further three armed officers rush into the room.

ALAN (CONT'D)
Yours, I believe. You probably thought I was gay when I gave you that cuddle. Don't worry, I'm not.

MASKED COP 1
You're really cool, Alan.

MASKED COP 2
Yes, we think you're cool.

ALAN
Thank you. Sorry, who are you?

The cop pulls off his mask to reveal that he's actually Alan, too. He extends his hand.

```
MASKED COP 1
Jason Statham.
```

*The next cop takes off his mask, extends his hand. He's
Alan, too.*

```
MASKED COP 2
(American drawl)
Jason Bourne.
```

*Next cop does the same. It's Alan again, this time
with a big handlebar moustache and lipstick.*

```
MASKED COP 3
Jason Argonaut.*
```

```
ALAN
Jason Argonaut?
```

```
MASKED COP 3
Mm.
```

....

* We'd always liked the oddness of this scene, but it was only on the day
that we decided that the Alan who says 'Jason Argonaut' should also be
wearing red lipstick. Watching it back in the edit, the lipstick seemed to
help sell the bizarreness of the moment. To this day, Steve carries it
around with him wherever he goes.

Left and below: We shot a teaser trailer on the first day of the shoot. It was based on Alan running through a possible list of names for the film. Judging from Twitter, *Alpha Papa* was far less popular than *Colossal Velocity*.

The opening scene of the film, which we shot twice. In the original version, the main phone-in for that morning's show was 'Why did Herbie go bananas? What was the root cause of the Volkswagen's very public mental collapse?'

The calm before the storm. Alan has no idea what lies ahead of him as he works in his business centre (shed).

The old team reunited. The first time they'd all been together on screen since series two of *I'm Alan Partridge* over a decade ago. The scene was cut.

Left: Alan can't decide if he's attracted by Angela's oddness or repelled by it, despite later starting a relationship with her.

Above: The police station. Actually part of Norwich City Hall.

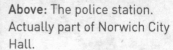

Colm Meaney as Pat Farrell. One of the original put-downs we had about him was 'Pat Farrell the fat barrel'. But when we then cast Meaney he was just too slender for it to work. Seriously, he's in great shape right now.

Left: 'I'll protect you.'

Above: Michael emerges from the cupboard with his lunchbox. 'Michael let himself down.' The contents were actually a mixture of cocoa powder, corn flour and dog shit.

An action hero clad in a leather jacket runs down a corridor.

Left: Alan talks to the police negotiator outside the radio station. We were originally going to shoot this scene with Alan shouting to the police (via loud hailer) from an upstairs window. Bringing it down to ground level gave us lots more options for the types of joke we could do. We improvised a lot of material for the bit of the scene where Alan turns his appearance into a stand-up comedy routine, before ditching it all in the edit.

Right: We came up with the station strap-line very early in the writing process. It was one of the few things that didn't change.

Danny Sinclair about to use the (fake) Taser on Nigel. In the background Michael eats a slice of (genuine) pizza.

The radio bus going through Norwich city centre. The crowds – including one woman from Japan – had turned out to see their idol in action.

Alan miming fear as he and Pat sing 'You're the Voice' by Jon Farnham.

Above and right:
Alan, moments
after shooting JFK.
'Oh, not again.'

Cromer Pier. Really pleased we chose this location. The faded glory
of the place worked well for our story. We very nearly ditched it in
favour of somewhere 'on land'.

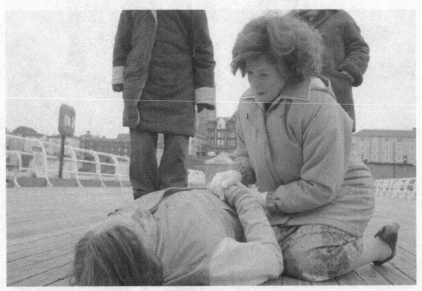

We only had Felicity for one afternoon of the Cromer shoot. She had
to race back to London because she was in a play with Ron Atkinson.
Or possibly Rowan Atkinson.

INT. RADIO STATION - CORRIDOR - DAY 3

Cut back to the corridor by the store room, where Alan was before the struggle began.

ALAN
It's Jason <u>and</u> the Argonauts.

We cut back to lipsticked, moustachioed cop for a second.

MASKED COP 3
Yeees.

And then back again.

PAT
You all right? You just said 'Clobber' and then 'Jason and the Argonauts'.

Alan realises it was a daydream.

ALAN
Oh, sorry.

PAT
All right. Shall we go?

ALAN
Yes.

PAT
Oh, by the way, thanks for not taking the gun.

ALAN
Oh, that's all right.

EXT. RADIO STATION – DAY 3

Over shots of the police and public outside the building, we hear Pat back on-air.

PAT
You're listening to Pat Farrell, and this is Willie Nelson, 'Always on My Mind', for someone who's always on my mind, my late wife Molly.

The song plays for a while.

The crowds are getting bigger. Quite a few of them are old, clearly Pat fans. We see some placards. 'Shape – the way we DON'T want it to be'. 'Attica'. 'Happy 40th, Lucy!!!!'

INT. SCHOOL/POLICE INCIDENT ROOM – DAY 3

The camera pans along the police intelligence board, across photos of the hostages, eventually stopping on one labelled 'Pat Farrell'. It's a picture of a smooth-chested male model. Janet looks hassled and is dishing out a bollocking to Sarge.

JANET
Does that man look 59 to you?

SARGE
I didn't look, I just put his name into Google
images.

*She grabs Pat's real photo from the table and slaps it
on the board.*

JANET
This is Pat Farrell. That is <u>a</u> Pat Farrell. Do I
have to do everything?

Steve Stubbs enters with the WPC.

STEVE STUBBS
Ma'am, you'd better hear this. It's taken from the
transcript of the broadcast.

The WPC reads from a transcript.

WPC
(Monotone)
01.00 hours. Partridge: I wish this was abroad,
because it would make a brilliant *Banged Up Abroad*.
Farrell: What's *Banged Up Abroad*? Partridge: You
don't know *Banged Up Abroad*? Farrell: No.
Partridge: Everyone knows *Banged Up Abroad*.
Farrell: I don't. What is *Banged Up Abroad*?
Partridge: You seriously don't know *Banged Up
Abroad*? You have to be shitting me. Farrell: I've
never heard of *Banged Up Abroad*. Partridge …

JANET
Get to the bit where they stop saying *Banged Up Abroad*.

The WPC skips forward a couple of pages.

WPC
Sidekick Simon: I once banged up a broad.
Partridge: That's the best you've got? Even with a gun to your head?

She stops reading.

JANET
He's got a gun to his head?

EXT. RADIO STATION – SIDE ALLEY – DAY 3

We see armed officers quietly approaching the back of the building.

INT. RADIO STATION – HOSTAGE ROOM – DAY 3

The hostages sit around, bored, while Dave monologues at them.

DAVE
I remember once coming to in a skip in the middle
of the afternoon with my underpants in my mouth,
and then I realised, hang on, these are not my
pants. Oh, I can laugh about it now, but back
then …

*There's the noise of movement coming through the wall
at the far end of the hostage room.*

EXT. RADIO STATION – DAY 3

The armed police are getting closer to the building.

INT. RADIO STATION – HOSTAGE ROOM – DAY 3

Connor is on his feet.

CONNOR
Shhh, what's that?

TONIA
It's the police.

*Alan walks in with some of the old canapés from the
party.*

ALAN
If you like canapés that are on the turn, you've
hit the motherlode. Oblong plate, square bowl, go
figure. Whatever happened to circles? I mean, I've
heard of a square meal, but that's ridiculous.

Dave laughs, so Alan tries to share it with the group.

ALAN (CONT'D)
I was just saying, I've heard of a square meal, but
that's …

JASON
Shhh!

ANGELA
We think it's the police.

*There's a scraping noise again. This time everyone
hears.*

CONNOR
That definitely came from in there.

*The hostages look at the wall. There's a palpable
sense of panic.*

JASON
Well, that's just a cupboard. It's not even an
outside wall.

ANGELA
No, Jason, don't!

ALAN
I'll protect you.

He puts his hand on her shoulders protectively, but gradually thinks better of it and ducks down behind her.

JASON
It's not an outside wall. Look, I'll show you. Look!

Unable to wait anymore, he yanks open the cupboard door and stands back. Everyone waits for a bang of some kind.

But it's just Michael, wearing a head lamp.

ALAN
Michael?

MICHAEL
Hello, Mr Partridge.

ALAN
What are you hiding in there for?

MICHAEL
Well, I found myself a place of concealment, like we're on manoeuvres.

ALAN
Michael, turn your light off. You're blinding everyone you speak to.

He presses the button, but it flashes intermittently.

DANNY
Now it's flashing.

MICHAEL
Oh, sorry.

He turns it off.

ALAN
Michael, you look like some sort of big Geordie
Anne Frank.* How long have you been here?

MICHAEL
All night.

ALAN
What did you eat?

MICHAEL
Well, I had my lunchbox.

ANGELA
Where did you go to the toilet?

ALAN
No ...

....

* Until the final take, this line had been: 'You look like some sort of big
Geordie mole.' Not good.

MICHAEL
I had my lunchbox.

They groan.

ALAN
Thank God it's got a smoky finish with an airtight
seal.

MICHAEL
I tell you what, they're right, mind. It seals in
the freshness.

ALAN
No, Michael, it seals out the freshness.

Pat bursts in, holding the gun.

PAT
What is going on in here?

ALAN
Oh, Pat, Michael's just visiting us from the
cupboard. No need to get shouty-shouty.

PAT
Did those Gordale bastards put you up to this?

JASON
No.

MICHAEL
No. No, no. I've been in here a few nights, like.

ALAN
Well, one night.

MICHAEL
No, a few nights. A few nights this week, a few
nights the week before.

ALAN
Why?

MICHAEL
Well, me brother wanted the bed to himself.

ALAN
Ah, yes. Michael suffers from night terrors. He
thrashes about like a big salmon.

PAT
What's in the box?

ALAN
Michael … Michael let himself down.

Michael approaches Pat solemnly.

MICHAEL
I'm really sorry. I done a shit in a box.

PAT
Well, get rid of it. Throw it out of the window!

Michael lobs it through the small gap.

EXT. RADIO STATION - SIDE ALLEY - DAY 3

The lunchbox crashes out of the building, just missing an armed officer. They're spooked, and retreat.

ARMED POLICEMAN
Fall back, fall back!

EXT. RADIO STATION - DAY 3

Martin waits 10 feet from the entrance. The automatic doors slide open. We can make out the silhouette of a man. The media and crowd fall silent.

Alan steps into the light. He's connected to a rope. Armed officers rush forward. *

....

* This scene was added to the script relatively late in the writing process. Until then we had no scenes of Alan interacting face to face with the police during the siege, nor did we have a way for Alan to see the scale of public interest for himself. So this is the key turning point in Alan's story, where he goes from hostage to bloke who realises this thing could be good for his career. It's what makes it an Alan story rather than a normal hostage story. Plus, on a more practical level, it breaks up the monotony of scene after scene in the confined space of the radio studio. Brilliantly shot by Ben Smithard.

The scene also contains a hidden *Dog Day Afternoon* reference. One of the home-made placards in the background reads 'Attica' (the name of the prison repeatedly mentioned by Pacino's character).

ARMED POLICEMAN
(Shouting)
Identify yourself, identify yourself!

ALAN
Alan Partridge! Alan Partridge! You know who I am,
I haven't been off the TV that long. Identify
yourself …

MARTIN
Alan, it's okay, I'm here. You're safe.

ALAN
Yes, tell them to stop, tell them to stop pointing
their guns at me.

MARTIN
Lower your weapons!

ALAN
Yes, lower your weapons.

One officer is still holding his gun.

ALAN (CONT'D)
Take your hand off your gun. Take your hand off
your gun, and the other hand. I can wait here all
day.

MARTIN
Do as he says.

ALAN
Thank you. Why did you have to turn it into a
competition? Just because I won.

Alan is tugged back towards the building.

ALAN (CONT'D)
Stop tugging me. I told you, I've a very sensitive
tummy.

MARTIN
Who are you talking to, Alan?

ALAN
I've got Pat on the end of the line in both senses.
I'm tethered to the building via this belly rope
and I'm relaying messages from Pat via this state-
of-the-art Sennheiser 1000 headset. Nice bit of
kit.

He puts his hand to his ear.

ALAN (CONT'D)
Yes, I'm telling them that now. If you'd listen
you'd know that I'm telling them. Right, Pat says
'Hi'.

MARTIN
Hi, Pat.

ALAN
And 'Hi' to your fellow officers.

POLICE OFFICERS
Hi, Pat.

MARTIN
Alan, listen — Pat works with us here, this can all
end well, okay? I give him my word.

Alan holds his hands up to shush him. Pat's talking.

ALAN
Okay, just — Pat, you're rambling. You've got to be
more concise, you know. What do you want? I want a
helicopter.
(To Martin)
That's just an example, by the way.
(Listens)
Okay. He wants a helicopter.

MARTIN
That might not be possible, Alan, but let's
dialogue. What else can we do?

EXT. RADIO STATION – REAR – DAY 3

*A bomb-disposal robot approaches the lunchbox. The
operator is several yards away, watching a monitor of
the robot's camera feed. Steve Stubbs is standing
behind him, watching intently. It reaches the box
and …*

EXT. RADIO STATION – DAY 3

BANG. The device is detonated. Alan flinches as the
police and public duck down and scream.

ALAN
Pat says, 'Fucking stupid pigs, what the hell's
going on?'

MARTIN
Pat, listen to me. That was not an attack, okay? We
just had to dispose of the box around the corner in
a controlled manner.

ALAN
Pat would prefer it if you spoke through me, as
would I.
(To Pat)
Martin says they deployed a remote RV fitted with a
disruptor to neutralise a suspected IED.
(To Martin)
He doesn't know what you're talking about. He's
actually quite angry. He's honking in my ear like a
mad Irish goose.

There's laughter from the crowd, and for the first time
Alan notices he has an audience.

FEMALE VOICES
We love you, Alan!

MALE VOICE
Aha!

ALAN
Do you mind? It's not a radio roadshow, I'm trying
to host a siege here.

FEMALE FAN
We love you, Alan!

ALAN
Get away!
(Unable to ignore it)
Who said that?

FEMALE FAN
What's it like in there?

ALAN
Scary, stressful, lots of shouting. A bit like
being married again.

The crowd laugh.

ALAN (CONT'D)
Oh, and there's a crazy person running around with
a gun, so it's a lot like being married again.

Another laugh. He starts to patrol the stage.

ALAN (CONT'D)
And when I saw a guy with a shotgun in his mouth,
begging for mercy, then I definitely …

A smaller laugh.

ALAN (CONT'D)
You're ahead of me. You're ahead of me, a lot of
you are.
No, I shouldn't laugh. Divorce is tough. 'Specially
on da man — don't get to see da kids.

MARTIN
Alan. Pat okay?

ALAN
He's good. He's laughing.

MARTIN
Okay. Laughter is good.

ALAN
He actually wants me to do a bit more …

He addresses the crowd again with even more gusto.

ALAN (CONT'D)
Has anyone got a cupboard in their house absolutely
full … of towels?

A few murmurs of recognition.

ALAN (CONT'D)
Everyone's got The Towel Cupboard, haven't they?
Everyone's got The Towel Cupboard! Y'know, what are
you gonna use them for? Are you expecting a big
army of men …? 'Oh, we are the big army of wet men!
All marching towards the house. Can we borrow your
towels?' Hardly likely! The woman of the house, she
always says, 'Oh, they're for guests!' Really? Who
are you expecting to turn up who's that wet?
Michael Phelps? The American gold-medallist
swimmer, often photographed wet …

The laughter's died away.

MARTIN
Alan?

ALAN
Yeah, sorry about that. He just said I should do
that. He thought it'd be good to lower the
temperature.
(To the crowd)
You guys were great, by the way …

MARTIN
Well, that may have been a good thing …

ALAN
I'll be here all week! Or I will be if the police
don't pull their finger out. He's still got his
hand on his gun. He thinks I don't know. Yeah, you,
I'm looking at you. Peripheral vision, mate.

MARTIN
Alan, we need to establish what it is that Pat
wants.

ALAN
Absolutely, Martin. Before I do that, quick big-up.
I don't know if you guys know who organised this?
Chief Constable Whitehead. Give it up!

The crowd applaud.

ALAN (CONT'D)
Yeah, but wait for it. She's a woman. Lot of people
say, 'Woman chief constable? Ridiculous!' Really?
Because when I look at her, I don't see a woman. I
just see a law enforcement officer who happens to
be damn attractive.*

ALAN (CONT'D)
(To the armed cop)
He's still got his hand on his gun. He thinks I
don't know. Yes, you, I'm looking at you.
Peripheral vision, mate.

MARTIN
Alan!

....

* This all worked but the scene was too long. And when a scene goes on
too long even funny stuff seems unfunny. And the towel stand-up felt
like a straight dig at Michael McIntyre, which wasn't necessarily the
intention.

Alan starts to walk backwards into the building.

ALAN
It's all right, I'm not retreating. Pat's tugging
me off.

People laugh. Alan is now inside the automatic doors.

ALAN (CONT'D)
Now come on, come on, we're better than that. Guys,
seriously ...

MARTIN
Alan, wait!

ALAN
Oh, by the way, there's an extra hostage. I meant
to tell you that!

The doors shut. He's gone.

BBC NEWS BROADCAST – MONTAGE – DAY 3

BBC NEWSCASTER
In a surprise development, DJ Alan Partridge
appeared outside the building, while tethered to a
rope.

BBC NEWSCASTER 2
Footage of his address is already one of the most
viewed YouTube videos since Fat Woman Falls Down
Hole.*

BBC NEWSCASTER
Mr Partridge, whose Facebook page lists one of his
interests as hand-to-hand combat, has been acting
as mediator between police and the hostage taker,
Pat Farrell.

Zoom in on Alan's publicity shot.

BBC NEWSCASTER 2
As people around the world ask, 'Who is Alan
Partridge?'

INT. RADIO STATION - STUDIO - DAY 3

Pat and Alan on-air, coming off the back of a song.

ALAN
That was a majestic voice. You can keep Jesus. As
far as I am concerned, Neil Diamond will always be
King of the Jews.

....

* This joke was added right at the end of the edit. We saw that the
earlier 'Fat Woman Falls Down Hole' scene worked, so this felt like an
obvious place for a call-back joke.

PAT
You were listening to …

JINGLE: 'The Partridge & The Poacher', followed by a squawk and a bang. Alan is now sitting next to Pat, in command of the desk, back at the top of his game.*

ALAN
And what I believe is a world first. I, Alan Partridge, a hostage, broadcasting live from a siege at gunpoint.

PAT
Pure class, Alan.

ALAN
And today we'll be asking: what was better in the olden days? Okay, Pat, shoot. I mean, start speaking.

INT. RADIO STATION – MONTAGE – DAY 3

Music: 'Enola Gay', OMD. Shots of the pair broadcasting are intercut with radios in and around Norwich.

....

* This whole scene – as we cut from location to location while listening to snippets of Alan's broadcast – was originally several stand-alone scenes. But after we'd done a few cuts of the film it become obvious that this was a place where the pace sagged. So we butchered the stand-alone scenes and turned them into a montage to inject a bit of energy.

PAT
Terry, in Necton.

TERRY
(On phone)
Egypt.

ALAN
I'm liking this.

TERRY
(On phone)
They used to build the pyramids and now they can't
even get you a taxi to the airport.

ALAN
Terry, I like the way you think, please do call
again.

TERRY
(On phone)
Will do.

ALAN
Nicholas, in Weybourne.

NICHOLAS
(On phone)
Nurses were better in the old days.

ALAN
Bull's eye.

PAT
Yes, they used to be these Florence Nightingale-
type figures.

ALAN
And these days it's just short-haired women in
trousers washing their own hands at a sink.

ALAN (CONT'D)
Okay, later on I'll be asking which vegetable has
the greatest torsional strength, i.e. which can
withstand the greatest twisting load before
rupture?

PAT
Caroline, in Sprowston.

CAROLINE
(On phone)
Beards were better in the olden days.

ALAN
Love it.

PAT
Sebastian, in Holt?

SEBASTIAN
(On phone)
UK manufacturing.*

....
* This character is the only Brummie in the film.

ALAN
Good. Good, but dull. Paul, in East Runcton.

PAUL
(On phone)
Kill them all, Pat. And shoot the women first.

Alan cuts him off.

ALAN
We'll also be asking: have you ever met a genuinely
clever bus driver?

INT. RADIO STATION - HOSTAGE ROOM - DAY 3

*The hostages look bored. Some are sleeping. Angela is
reading, Connor is drumming on his thigh and Jason is
listening to the show.*

JASON
I wonder what the listening figures are for this.

DAVE
Can you stop drumming?

INT. RADIO STATION - STUDIO - DAY 3

Pat and Alan are still on-air.

PAT
Okay. Time for fact of the day.

JINGLE: 'Fact of the day, sponsored by Norfolk Dairies'. Followed by a loud moo.*

SIMON
Cows don't have hymens.

ALAN
Absolutely correct. Cows do not have hymens, just a partially open cervix. The time is 10:22. Right, now to your muster stations, it's Bryan Ferry.†

And they're off-air.

ALAN (CONT'D)
Ah, that, that was … radio gravy.

PAT
Wow.

Alan looks at Simon.

ALAN
I suppose you forget about the gun after a while, don't you?

....

* In the edit we asked for the sound of mooing cows at the end of this jingle to be pushed right up in the mix, until it almost assaults your eardrums. Somehow that made it funnier.

† This was a song intro we originally wrote for Mid Morning Matters. A dull footnote, that.

SIMON
No.

ALAN
Okay.

PAT
Good.

EXT. RADIO STATION/POLICE CORDON – DAY 3

Lynn tries to walk past the media.

JOURNALIST
Lynn? Lynn Benfield, can we have a word?

LYNN
Alan doesn't like me speaking to the press.

JOURNALIST
But we're not press, we're television.

LYNN
Well, I'm not really …

She touches her hair.

JOURNALIST
We've got hair and make-up.

Beat.

LYNN
Oh.

INT. RADIO STATION - HOSTAGE ROOM - DAY 3

Alan is in the hostage room. There's a swagger about him, largely because he's currently on the TV.

BBC NEWSCASTER
Back now to Norwich, where DJ Alan Partridge continues to bring news …

ALAN
(Playfully)
Angela? Someone wants a word with you.

ANGELA
Who?

ALAN
Him.

He nods towards the TV, but by the time Angela looks round, he's no longer on-screen. It's Kim Jong-un.

ANGELA
Why?

He looks up.

ALAN
Oh, shit.

Alan flicks through dozens and dozens of channels at high speed. The camera stays on his face and his expression goes from contentment to confusion to irritation to mounting concern. Eventually, he finds a channel where he's on.

ALAN (CONT'D)
Him! Look — me, on the TV. Good photo.

INT. RADIO STATION — DISABLED TOILET — DAY 3

Alan leads Angela into a disabled toilet, trying to act breezy.

ALAN
Yeah, it's just your basic disabled loo. You've got your lowered seat pan, back pad, hi-vis grab bar, panic cord, lady bin …

ANGELA
Alan, calm down, you're being all hectic. This is because you're on TV, isn't it? You're all puffed up like a robin.

ALAN
It's like you can see in me …

ANGELA
Alan, you didn't bring me in here to talk about disabled toilet facilities, did you?

ALAN
Yeah, I did.
(Beat)
No, I didn't.

EXT. RADIO STATION – DAY 3

Lynn emerges from a make-up trailer.

JOURNALIST
Oh, wow. Lynn, you look fantastic.

*The journalist hands Lynn a mirror. She looks at
herself and seems surprised. She has volumised hair
and colour in her cheeks.*

LYNN
Good gracious.

INT. RADIO STATION – DISABLED TOILETS – DAY 3

Angela and Alan are standing very close to each other.

ALAN
You know, I have this mad dream where the two of us
have a day out in the Scottish Highlands. And we're
standing on this craggy rock – well, more of a
rocky crag – just staring out majestically and
roaring into the abyss.

ANGELA
Just shouting, 'Scotland!'

ALAN
Yeah. Or I prefer, 'The UK!'

ANGELA
And what else did we do?

ALAN
We laid on the grass, looking up at the sky,
pretending to be Scottish people and laughing our
heads off.

ANGELA
We 'lay' on the grass.

ALAN
No, I was using the past tense. Laid on the grass.

ANGELA
I know, but 'lay' is the intransitive past tense of
'lie'.

This sinks in.

ALAN
Oh, yeah. Where are you from? The …

ANGELA
Ipsw—

```
ALAN
Wait ...! The Planet Knockout?
```

```
ANGELA
Ipswich.
```

She moves closer.*

She's clearly about to kiss him. There's a whistle from his nose.

```
ALAN
I'm sorry about the nasal whistle. It's when I'm
anxious.†
```

It whistles again but she puts a finger on his nostril to silence it. And with her finger still there, she kisses him noisily.

Eventually, he breaks away to speak.

```
ALAN (CONT'D)
Mm. You know 'Shape — the way you want it to be'?
```

....

* A chunk that worked on the page, worked on the day, looked ropey in the edit. Sometimes that happens.

† The nasal whistle is what eventually reveals Alan's identity to Pat as he hides in the loo on the bus. It had only appeared in this scene originally, but we figured it'd be good to turn it into a runner that ends up costing Alan. Naturally, we had many arguments about the pitch and volume of the whistle.

ANGELA
Yes.

ALAN
Well, your shape's the way I want it to be. I'm on
about your body.

She looks down at his groin.

ANGELA
And what might this be?

ALAN
That is my damn todger, and it's all the fault of a
certain Miss Angela ... I'm sorry, I don't know your
second name.

INT. RADIO STATION – HOSTAGE ROOM – DAY 3

*Jason is watching the TV in the hostage room as Lynn
gives an interview to camera.*

LYNN
He's very brave. He was once feeding ducks in the
park. One took a peck at him, and instead of
retreating he hit it with the back of his hand. He
just rapped its bill.

*Jason looks through, sees Alan in the studio and
beckons him in.*

JASON
Hi!

ALAN
Hey!

JASON
Got time for a quick waah-waah?

Alan looks at him blankly.

JASON (CONT'D)
A quick waah-waah?

ALAN
Oh, you mean 'wa-wa'?

JASON
Yes.

ALAN
Sorry. You just did a different noise.

JASON
Look, how are you feeling about this, this whole
media circus? How are you feeling?

ALAN
Between you and me, pretty puffed up, like … an
owl.

JASON
Well, let's hope you're a wise one.

ALAN
Nice. I pitched it up, you knocked it out of the
park.
(Interlocking his fingers)
Synergy. Oh, no, that's lesbians.

JASON
Let me tell you something, Alan. As far as the
press is concerned, you are the face of this siege.

ALAN
I am Siege Face.

JASON
Exactly. After this, you'll get more offers than a
whore at our Christmas party!

ALAN
(Laughing bawdily)
I like that!

JASON
Yes, you'd know a thing or two about that, wouldn't
you?

ALAN
That would be …
(Twirls imaginary moustache)
That's a moustache.

JASON
Seriously, did you give her one?

ALAN
Well, I gave her a ruddy big kiss she won't forget
in a hurry. Hand on the outside of the bra —
reconnaissance — and then I just held her in my
arms, because she told me she never knew her
mother. And I said, 'Well, my mother raised me and
lived to a ripe old age, but — guess what? — I
never really knew her, and …'
(Composing himself)
To get back on track, yes. Woo!

JASON
I like you.

ALAN
(Instantly)
I like you.

INT. RADIO STATION – CORRIDOR – DAY 3

*Alan is talking to Lynn on the phone as he strides
down the corridor. Intercut with Lynn at home.*

ALAN
He likes me, Lynn. Jason Tresswell likes me.*

LYNN
Alan, are you okay?

ALAN
I've got to be quick. Pat only thinks I've borrowed
his phone to play Angry Birds on the toilet.

LYNN
Of course. What is it?

ALAN
It's a computerised bird-throwing game.

LYNN
No, I meant …

ALAN
I'm joking, Lynn! Enjoy me. Everyone else is.
Gordale Media think I'm some sort of Christ 2.0. Do
you know, I'm within a brair's headth of getting
the breakfast show? I'm going to call myself the
morning rooster, or the talking cock.

....

* We reshot this scene, less on comedy grounds and more on story
grounds. Alan had been almost laid-back in the first go at it. You got no
sense that Jason buttering him up in the previous scene had excited him,
nor did you get a sense that Alan knew he needed the siege to keep
going if it was going to help his career. Thus there was less of an 'Oh,
shit' moment when he accidentally escapes.

LYNN
Alan, you're not thinking clearly.

ALAN
Yes, I am. Lynn, I'll say this once and I'll say it
again. My career is getting a shot in the arm from
this siege, and if I can stay in here until the
bitter end, I will be the biggest thing to come out
of Norwich since Lord Nelson, or Trisha. Think
about that, Lynn. Think about what that means.

LYNN
Your first priority should be the welfare of the
hostages.

ALAN
That's good. Put that out as a press release and
say I said it.

LYNN
Alan, your ego's getting the better of you.

ALAN
I've just got to stay alert and focused. I'm
playing them like an oboe, Lynn. How effed up is
that?

*As Alan says this he pushes through a door. It closes
behind him.*

EXT. RADIO STATION - REAR - DAY 3

It takes a second to sink in, then he looks at the
door. It was a fire exit at the back of the building.
He's outside. He pulls at the door, trying to get back
in. It won't open.

  ALAN
  Oh.

Looking around, Alan sees a ground-floor bathroom
window slightly ajar. He climbs over the fire-escape
railings so he can approach it from above and opens
the window to slide his legs in first.

He gets his balance wrong, though, and ends up jammed
in the small opening like a stuck pig. Legs inside,
body outside, hinging at the waist. His belt is caught
on the window latch.

  ALAN (CONT'D)
  Not now! Oh, for God's sake. I'm caught on the
  latch.

He accepts that he needs to gets his legs out and try
again, so he lets his body fall. His legs follow, and
his trousers and underpants start to come off.

  ALAN (CONT'D)
  Come on, please!

Eventually, his trousers and underpants are off
completely. He gets up from the floor and reaches for
his trousers.

ARMED POLICEMAN
Stop! Armed police. Get your hands above your head.

Alan turns to see an armed officer pointing a gun at
him. He covers his genitals with one hand and tries to
grab his trousers with the other.

ALAN
I can't … I've just …

ARMED POLICEMAN
Get your hands above your head!

ALAN
I just want to get those trousers.

ARMED POLICEMAN
Do it! Get your hands above your head. Do it!

ALAN
They're my trousers.

ARMED POLICEMAN
Get your hands above your head, now.

Alan hesitates and then puts them up. He's tucked his
penis between his legs.

ARMED POLICEMAN (CONT'D)
What are you doing? It's weird.

ALAN
There are paparazzi all over the place and I do not
want them to get a photograph of my genitals.

*At that moment, a photographer emerges out of nowhere
and snaps him from behind.*

ALAN (CONT'D)
Ah, come on!

He turns to glare at the guy.

PHOTOGRAPHER
That's it! Look at me.

*Eventually, the photographer finishes snapping him and
walks off.*

INT. SCHOOL/POLICE INCIDENT ROOM – DAY 3

*Alan wears paper forensic trousers. He is being
debriefed by Janet and Martin.*

MARTIN
And how were the hostages when you left?

ALAN
Crouched, brave, big.

MARTIN
I mean, what's their state of mind?

ALAN
If I'm honest, a bit moany. Is someone writing this
down?

An officer in the corner raises his hand.

ALAN (CONT'D)
Oh, sorry. I thought you were some clothes. Thanks
for the forensic trousers, by the way.

MARTIN
Could you just …?

He signals for him to sit with his legs closed.

ALAN
Oh, crikey! Yes, sorry. I was going to fashion a
sort of makeshift modesty sporran from the vacant
arm flaps.

*He crams the arm flaps under his buttocks to block the
view, then looks up.*

JANET
Okay, I think we're done here.

ALAN
Any chance of freshening up? I just need to wipe my
face with a big hot towel, and presumably you want
to use me as part of your media strat?

JANET
No.

ALAN
Do you agree?

MARTIN
Hundred per cent.

ALAN
Got you.

He marches out confidently, to save face.

INT. ALAN'S LOUNGE - NIGHT 3

Alan's sat watching TV, looking despondent. On-screen is the rolling news of the siege. Lynn is with him.

LYNN
The police said you could do media interviews when the siege is over.

He stands up and walks across the room.

ALAN
It'll be too late then, Lynn. People move on.
Gordale Media'll move on.

LYNN
But you're still being talked about.

ALAN
Only because every time I look at the telly they're
showing a picture of my arse.

Behind Alan, on TV, Lynn's face is on-screen. Whenever
Alan mentions his backside, Lynn appears. And vice
versa.

ALAN (CONT'D)
It's all right for you. Every other time I look
they're showing a picture of your face, and then
the next time — surprise, surprise — my arse again.

LYNN
I mean, I was only telling people about you.

ALAN
You know, I was Gordale's golden goose and now I'm
just partridge pie ... with peas.

LYNN
But why do you want to work for people like that?
Gordale are bullies.

ALAN
Yes, and what do you do with a bully, then? You
make friends with the bully so they bully someone
else.

LYNN
'What doth it profit a man ...'

ALAN
Doth?

LYNN
'... if he gains the whole world yet loses his soul?'
Matthew, chapter eight ...

ALAN
Yes, I know who wrote it. I'm not going to sell my
soul, Lynn. I want to, if you like, lend my soul to
Gordale Media on a long-term basis for cash. It's a
very different thing. It, it, it ...

*Unable to think of a point to make, he just stares her
out.*

LYNN
I don't know how you can look yourself in the eye.

ALAN
I can't, Lynn. My nose is in the way. And you can
talk, prattling away on every news bulletin. I
mean, who the heck do you think you are?

LYNN
(Defiantly)
I'm Lynn Benfield.

ALAN
You don't look like Lynn Benfield. I mean, what has
happened to you? With your attitude and your hair,
you've literally become a big head.

LYNN
I like it.

ALAN
I take no pleasure in saying this, Lynn, but a lot
of people think it looks like a photograph of an
explosion.

LYNN
I don't know if I want to work for a man like you.

ALAN
I don't know that I want to employ someone who
looks like a madam. And I don't mean a Parisian
one, I mean one who lives in a terraced house
behind a train station.

*Lynn's had enough. She storms off, leaving Alan alone
with his nasal whistle.*

EXT. RADIO STATION – DAY 4

The automatic doors open.

ARMED POLICEMAN
Armed police, stay where you are! Armed police!

Pat emerges with the gun to Simon's head.

PAT
Just shut up, will you? Stop shouting.

MARTIN
Easy, Pat. Mind the steps.

PAT
I'm able to walk down steps, all right?

SIMON
I think he means because the gun's against my head.

PAT
Everybody has an opinion, huh?

ALAN
(Off)
Hear, hear. Well said.

Pat looks over and sees Alan at the cordon. Martin glances over in quiet panic — who let him in here?

ALAN (CONT'D)
Hi, Pat!

PAT
Hey, Alan. What happened? We were in the middle of a show and the next thing your arse is all over the internet.

SIMON
Looked like you had a turkey's head between your legs.

People laugh.

ALAN
No, it didn't. Doesn't have a beak and, yes, I took
an executive decision to stow my cock and balls up
against my backside.

*Alan looks at the old woman next to him, then back at
Pat.**

PAT
I can't believe you left me with this nutcase.

SIMON
Hang on a minute, you're the one with the gun,
mate.

PAT
See? He's hilarious.

ALAN
He's solid, he's solid.

MARTIN
(To wrestle the focus back)
Pizzas coming through now, Pat.

*Martin nods at the pizza-delivery guy to go forward.
Before he's even past the cordon, Pat speaks again.*

....

* The idea of Alan realising he's standing next to a little old lady only
came to us late in the day, so some lucky member of the production staff
got the task of 'sourcing' an old lady at short notice.

PAT
Hey, hey, hey, hold on! Helmet off.

There's a moment's hesitation, then the delivery guy puts his helmet on the floor. As he moves forward he goes past Alan and catches his eye.

ALAN
Oh, hello.

We now see that the pizza guy is actually Don from the TFU. Don's face tells Alan he should keep his mouth shut. Pat sees this little moment and dwells on it as Don advances. When he's halfway, Pat speaks up.

PAT
Actually, I want Alan to bring them in.

MARTIN
That might not be possible, Pat. Alan's not prepared to do that.

ALAN
No, I am prepared to do that.

MARTIN
It's not that simple, Pat.

Alan's already crossed the cordon.

PAT
Do you want me to release some people?

MARTIN
Sure, let's talk about that.

PAT
Alan, what do you reckon? Will I let the women go?

ALAN
Yes, let a couple of the women go. Maybe keep
Angela?

PAT
No, but her kids will be worried sick.

ALAN
She's got kids?

PAT
Yes, two boys, 14 and 15. I believe they're a real
handful.

Pause.

ALAN
Yes, what was I thinking? Let all the women go.

MARTIN
Okay, Pat, just give me five minutes with head
office.

PAT
He's bringing them in now. Alan, come on.

He jabs the gun forward, nudging Simon hard, silencing
Martin. Alan takes the pizzas and Don whispers to him.

DON
Top one.

ALAN
What?

STEVE STUBBS
Top one.

ALAN
Yes, yes, cheers, guys. Top one.

INT. RADIO STATION – FOYER – DAY 4

Alan and Pat are in the doorway. Alan is holding the
pizzas and leading the way, happy to be back in there.
But Pat stops.

PAT
Why did you say hello to that delivery guy?

ALAN
Oh, him. He just reminded me of a man I know called
Mike Cable, who did my accounts from '97 to '98.
Actually, no, '99 … until he stopped because his
daughter was very ill. Yes, it was touch and go,
actually. He and Sandra were in bits. Had to cancel
their holiday. It was a fly-drive to Tuscany. I
must tell him, actually, that there's a policeman
that looks just, just like him.

PAT
What's that?

ALAN
I must tell Mike that there's a pizza man who looks
just like him. I am famished.

INT. RADIO STATION – HOSTAGE ROOM – DAY 4

*Alan enters the hostage room with Pat. Everyone looks
up, unsure what's going on but too wary to speak.*

PAT
Ladies, you're free to go!

*Tonia says a brief goodbye to Connor, and then she,
Chastity and Angela head to the door. Angela stops in
front of Alan.*

ANGELA
I'll make you a home-made pizza when you get out.

ALAN
Yes, these pizzas are pretty good.

She picks up her shoe and holds it up.

ANGELA
Cinderella.

ALAN
Well, that was a glass one, wasn't it?

The women leave and Alan opens the top pizza box. It has a Taser in it. He shuts it quickly. Pat comes over.

ALAN (CONT'D)
Just trying to find your pizza.

PAT
Just give me that one.

ALAN
Mm?

PAT
That one.

ALAN
Which one?

PAT
The top one!

ALAN
(Penny drops)
Oh.

Dave takes the pizzas over while Alan tries to think straight. Jason whispers to him.

JASON
Thanks for coming back, Alan.

Jason holds up his fingers, as if framing Alan in a photo.

ALAN
What are you doing?

JASON
Just seeing how you'll look on the billboard. For when you start on *Breakfast*.

ALAN
(Suddenly interested)
The Breakfast Show?

PAT
(Off)
Alan? Can I have a word?

ALAN
Yes, sure, just bringing the pizza cutter. Right, how many do you want, six or eight?

*Pat opens the pizza box and Alan tries to feign
surprise.*

ALAN
Oh, my God, that's a Taser! This is no use. It's a
pizza cutter and that is not a pizza. Thing is, how
did it get there? Unless the pizza company are
running some sort of competition in which you win a
Taser ... That doesn't make sense, does it? No, it's
the police, isn't it? Do you know, they've got some
brass neck for a bunch of coppers. I'm actually
really angry about that. You should keep that as an
extra weapon, frankly, after the ...

PAT
(Snapping)
What kind of fool do you take me for, eh? I'm one
step ahead of all of you!

JASON
And I'm just a step behind you, mate.

*They look round. Jason is holding the gun. In the
chaos, Pat had left it unattended. Jason motions for
him to move away from the box. Danny picks up the
Taser.*

JASON (CONT'D)
Never take your eye off the ball, Pat. First rule
of business. Second rule of business: always be
prepared for an opportunity when it arises, like I
was just then. Of course, I wouldn't expect you to
understand that, it's Darwinian. You're a runt.

PAT
Is that what you think, Alan?

ALAN
I wouldn't quite, you know, use those words, but I think the gist is …

PAT
I just don't like bullies.

SIMON
(Meaning the tape)
Can I take this off, please?

PAT
Yes, yes, sure.

SIMON
No, I'm talking to him.
(Jason)

PAT
Oh, for fuck's sake.

JASON
Yes, go ahead.

SIMON
Thank you.

Connor comes over to help free Simon.

CONNOR
Are you all right?

SIMON
Well, I was worried about me old head, but I think
I've got a handle on it!

JASON
Alan's a smart cookie, Pat. He's treated this whole
crisis like a business opportunity. He's taken a
look around him and he's thought, how can I make
this work for me? Well done, Alan.

ALAN
Cheers.

PAT
Yes, well done, Alan.

ALAN
Thank you.

*Alan is fidgeting. The camera slowly zooms in on him as
Jason speaks, intercut with Pat slumped on a chair,
despondent.*

JASON
You know, you and me, we've got something going
here. Pat might be a dinosaur filling his show with
chit-chat and phone-ins like it's 1983, but you're
one of us. You know radio's just business. You'll
do well out of this and I'll get you a glamorous
assistant with big tits to take over from that
frumpy old cow you've got at the moment — you know,
Mrs fucking Doubtfire.

Alan doesn't like this.

ALAN
Danny? Jason gave me your *Breakfast* show.

DANNY
Is that true?

JASON
Well …

DANNY
You twat.

*Jason is about to justify it but Danny tasers him and
he falls to the ground. Connor, Dave and Simon rush to
help Jason.* Danny stands there in shock.*

INT. SCHOOL/POLICE INCIDENT ROOM – DAY 4

*Alerted by Jason's scream, Steve Stubbs mobilises
several armed officers.*

STEVE STUBBS
Go, go, go!

INT. RADIO STATION – HOSTAGE ROOM – DAY 4

*Armed officers smash into the hostage room through a
window. The hostages cower, apart from Simon, who
kneels up in front of them.*

ARMED POLICEMAN
(Shouting)
Armed police, armed police! Everybody stay down!
Stay down! Don't move, don't move!

----

* In the original cut, Connor had seen that Jason needed bringing
round and shouted, 'Has anyone got any brandy?' Instantly, Dave
Clifton had replied, 'There's a bottle of whisky behind the microwave,'
revealing his teetotalism had been a sham all along. We cut it in the end.
It felt a bit cruel.

SIMON
(Shouting)
Have you got any scissors?! Have you got any
scissors?!

INT. RADIO STATION - HOSTAGE ROOM - DAY 4

Officers push open the studio door, ready to shoot. The
studio is empty.

ARMED POLICEMAN
Armed police, armed police! Studio empty! Where's
Farrell? Where's Partridge?

EXT. RADIO STATION - DAY 4

There's a whirring noise and the doors to the basement
ramp start to open.

An engine revs and we see the roadshow-mobile with its
garish, out-dated livery coming up the ramp.

EXT. FRONT OF BUILDING - DAY 4

Steve Stubbs emerges from the front entrance as the
bus comes into view. Alan is sitting at the radio desk
with his hands raised. Pat is pointing the gun at him.
Steve speaks over the radio.

STEVE STUBBS
Right, we've got three on a bus, three on a bus. I
want green light on a sniper, now.

Janet runs out from the incident room.

JANET
This cannot be happening.

INT. ROADSHOW BUS - FRONT OF BUILDING - DAY 4

*With his hands still raised, Alan looks out at the
armed police surrounding them.*

PAT
Jeez, Alan, look at this. Quite alarming, isn't it?

ALAN
I think we'll be fine.

PAT
Thanks for doing this, Alan. I just wanted to stick
it to Gordale one more time.

ALAN
I don't mind in the slightest, Pat. Gordale are
tits.

Michael is driving, clearly enjoying himself.

MICHAEL
Right, coppers, I've got no tax, no insurance and
I'm not wearing a seat belt, and what are you going
to do about it this time?

EXT. RADIO STATION/ROADSHOW BUS – DAY 4

*Outside the bus police run to their cars, armed guys
struggle into a minibus in their bulky kit, reporters
report and some people try to run along with the bus.*

*The bus has come up against a parked police car. There
doesn't look to be enough room to get through.*

*There's not enough room to get past the parked police
cars, but Michael just shunts them out of the way with
a crunch.*

INT. GRUBBY OFFICE – DAY 4

*CECIL, a seedy man in his sixties, is sitting behind a
desk, reading Lynn's CV in silence. There's no chair
for her.*

LYNN
I've not seen you at church recently.

CECIL
No, I stopped going.

Lynn expects him to expand on this. He doesn't. He looks up.

CECIL (CONT'D)
Well, you certainly seem to have the required skill set for the position.

Lynn smiles sadly.

CECIL (CONT'D)
And I hope you're not averse to making coffee, as it's a drink I enjoy.

LYNN
Not at all.

CECIL
In that case, pop the kettle on now while I take a shower.

He hands her the CV and walks to the door. She bends down to pick up her bag. He watches her.

CECIL (CONT'D)
There will be some weekend work.

LYNN
Fine. I like to keep busy.

CECIL
(Still watching her bend over)
That's what I've always admired about you, Lynn. Your diligence.

She stands up. He looks away and leaves. *

EXT. FRONT OF BUILDING – DAY 4

A bunch of police cars, an ambulance and media vehicles gradually form a convoy and trail along behind the bus as it trundles away from the building.

PAT
Right! Let's give them some stick.

They fade up their mics.

ALAN
You're listening to Pat and Alan with a message for the Gordale Medias of this world. If you think you can take real DJs and turn them into radio robots, think again, because we're going to get up in your face with a big fat slice of roadshow radio, right here, right now. The time is 1:27. This is John Farnham and The Voice.

....

* This was probably the hardest scene to cut. Lovely to see Lynn actually on the point of getting a job away from Alan, but you were also willing her not to do it because Cecil was such a dirty old git. There was real relief when she heard Alan on the radio, realised he'd done the right thing and fled to be by his side. But we needed really frenetic pacing when the roadshow bus broke out of the station and headed to Cromer, and going to this scene in the middle of all that killed the pace totally.

ALAN PARTRIDGE: ALPHA PAPA

*Alan takes the sign from the window that bears the
name of the last DJ to have used it. He flips it over
and writes 'Pat & Alan' on the back. He puts it up.*

EXT. NORWICH TOWN CENTRE – DAY 4

*The convoy drives slowly along in front of the
Millennium Building and onto the road by City Hall.*

ALAN
Today I'll be asking: why do people keep their eggs
in the fridge? Once again, why do people insist on
keeping their eggs in the fridge? Oh, and can a bin
man reasonably expect a Christmas tip when he has
point-blank refused to dispose of a broken toaster?

PAT
Good question.

ALAN
And that can be today's Large Question.

JINGLE: 'Large Question!'

177

EXT. COUNTRY LANE – DAY 4

*A wide, open Norfolk vista. A country road, trees, a
big sky. From the right the broadcast bus trundles
into shot. As we hear Alan talk, we see the bus is
being followed by numerous emergency services
vehicles, then media vehicles. They're travelling at
O. J. Simpson speed.*

PAT
Oh, and we have some travel news. There's slow-
moving traffic on the A149.

ALAN
That'll be due to whacky blokes on a big yellow
bus!

They high-five.

EXT. NEAR SHERINGHAM – DAY 4

Alan is hosting a phone-in.

ALAN
It's competition time, and we're playing pairs. Sid
on line 2. Black and …

SID
Decker.

ALAN
Spick and …

SID
Span.

ALAN
Hall and ...

SID
Oates.

ALAN
Egg and ...

SID
Bacon.

ALAN
Ohhhh, it was gammon.

SID
Can I just say, I think Gordale are awful?

PAT
Yes, they are bastards.

ALAN
Pat, that's why I've washed my hands of them. You
know what I always say. I always say: what doth it
profit a man if he gain the whole world yet loothe
his soul?

INT. GRUBBY OFFICE - KITCHEN - DAY 4

Lynn is making coffee in Cecil's dirty kitchen. The radio is on and she hears Alan.

ALAN
And people seem to like that, they really do.

Lynn's eyes widen with joy.

INT. LYNN'S HOUSE - DAY 4

Lynn has the radio on and looks up when she hears this.

ALAN
And people seem to like that, they really do.

Lynn smiles.

EXT. SHERINGHAM HIGH STREET - DAY 4

John Farnham's chorus kicks in. The streets are lined with supporters, some holding banners, others cheering them on.

Alan mimes along to the words, in his element.

ALAN
Looks like you've touched a nerve, Pat.

PAT
These are my listeners, Alan, ordinary working
people.

ALAN
Yes. Well, they're not working, it's the middle of
the day, unless they're on flexi-time.

INT. GRUBBY OFFICE - KITCHEN - DAY 4

Cecil enters, wearing a silk kimono.

CECIL
I should also add that I like to let the skin
breathe after a good wash, so I hope you're not …

He stops. Lynn is gone.

EXT. APPROACHING THE COAST - DAY 4

Still on-air, Alan notices a static-caravan site.

ALAN
Oh, look, I used to live in one of those after my
divorce. TV, kitchen, very nice.

INT. ROADSHOW BUS - DAY 4

Alan continues to rant while Pat looks at the Gordale Media website and a picture of the board members Alan addressed earlier.

> ALAN
> Hey, people, I'm looking at a picture of Gordale Media. Honestly, look at that bunch of corporate mercenaries.

But Pat has seen something. In the background, near the people posing, is the whiteboard on which Alan wrote the words 'Just sack Pat'.

> ALAN (CONT'D)
> What's wrong with doing radio for the love of radio? They would do anything for 30 pieces of silver. You're listening to the Pat and Alan Show, radio for the love of radio.

JINGLE: 'Sponsored by Castrol!'

But Pat isn't listening. He has the photo and the 'Pat & Alan' sign from the bus window side by side. Alan sees Pat comparing the handwriting.

> ALAN (CONT'D)
> Just need the loo.

Alan gets up and goes to the toilet, ignoring the 'Out of Order' sign on the door.

INT. ROADSHOW BUS/TOILET – DAY 4

Fearing he's been rumbled, Alan locks the door.

Outside, Pat hammers on the toilet door.

PAT
Alan!

ALAN
Hi!

Alan is looking around desperately for a way out. He eyes up the small opaque window to gauge if he can get through.

PAT
Alan? I want to talk to you. Alan!

There's a clanking noise. Pat forces open the door. Alan's gone. The window is open.

As he peers out to look for Alan, there's the sound of nasal whistling. It's coming from the toilet.

Pat lifts the toilet lid. Alan's face is peering up from the toilet. He's lying on his back in the tank.

ALAN
Oh. Hi, Pat.

PAT
Alan, how did you even get in there?

ALAN
I just removed an aluminium panel, slid straight
in. Textbook. It's good, isn't it?

PAT
Your voice sounds funny.

ALAN
I think the conical shape of the toilet's turned it
into a sort of compact amphitheatre.

PAT
It's weird.

ALAN
It is, Pat, it's bizarre. It is and was a failed
escape attempt, a sort of Shitshank Redemption, if
you will.

PAT
The Armitage Shank Redemption.

ALAN
(Laughing too hard)
I'm laughing like a drain, Pat, and I'm in one.
Shake hands, Pat, friends. Friends, Pat, friends.

His hand comes out of the toilet. Pat knocks it away.

PAT
Friends? I know what you did, you fucking snake.
Just sack Pat? You're as bad as the rest of them.

ALAN
Pat, be reasonable. Before you think of shooting
anyone, just for a second think what would drive a
man to incarcerate himself in a septic tank? It's
absolutely pathetic.

PAT
I'm not going to shoot you.

ALAN
Thank God for that.

Pat starts undoing his belt.

ALAN (CONT'D)
Mother of God, no! Oh, angels and saints preserve
us. Dear God, let them be firm!

*Alan's weight causes the tank to come away and he ends
up on the road outside Cromer's Hotel de Paris.*

Pat leans out the window.

PAT
Stop the bus!

EXT. HOTEL/INT. ROADSHOW BUS — DAY 4

*Alan climbs out of the tank. On the pavement a woman
is looking at him.*

PASSER-BY
What's that?

ALAN
It's a septic tank. You can have it.

He runs.

On the bus, Michael slams the breaks on and Pat almost loses his footing. He regains his balance and manages to get off the bus, but Alan has a decent head start on him.

EXT. HOTEL/INT. STEVE STUBBS'S CAR - DAY 4

The police pull up and see Pat running after Alan.

EXT. PIER - DAY 4

Alan flees onto the pier in audible panic. On either side of the pier are two huts, covered in tarpaulin for the winter.

Alan checks Pat can't see, then enters one.

Now on the pier, Pat closes the gate behind him and puts the padlock on.

INT. SHOOTING GALLERY - DAY 4

*Alan finds himself in a shooting gallery. He breaks in
and finds a rifle. He grabs a handful of pellets and
aims the gun through the gap in the tarpaulin.*

*Pat stalks down the pier and we see Alan's POV. Pat
doesn't know which of the two huts Alan is in. With
Pat now in his sights, Alan pulls the trigger, but his
shot misses Pat by a good 10 yards, hitting a man on a
poster (JFK) right between the eyes. Alan looks
guilty.**

> ALAN
> Oh, not again.
> (Looking at the rifle)
> Damn gypsies tampered with the sights.

*He reloads and we see his POV again as he aims way to
the left of Pat, right between the eyes of a Susan
Boyle poster.*

....

* This idea started with Alan accidentally shooting Susan Boyle. That
felt like too cheap a shot, so we moved Susan to later in the joke ('Trust
me, Susan'). At first we replaced her with Uri Geller (we were looking
for someone international, someone who still felt Alan-y, but also
someone who the viewer might almost feel deserved to be the butt of
this joke). In the end we went with a different take on it, the idea of
shooting someone who'd already famously been shot. That felt like a far
better way to go.

ALAN (CONT'D)
(Whispers)
Trust me, Susan.

He fires, and Pat is hit on the ear. He cries out in pain.

Alan un-cocks the gun so it hangs over his arm. Pat is looking at the rifle hut and starts heading over.

Alan leaves with the gun.

EXT. PIER – DAY 4

Pat clutches his ear in pain, then grits his teeth and pursues Alan again.

EXT. ENTRANCE TO PIER – DAY 4

Armed cops have got past the bus that blocked their way and are coming down the pier. Lynn pulls up abruptly, gets out of her car and follows.

EXT. END OF PIER – DAY 4

Alan makes a circuit of the pavilion theatre and comes out the other side. No sign of Pat. He creeps to the corner to check for Pat, then turns as if he's heard something. He creeps back, then stops and creeps back again. He repeats this one too many times.

PAT
(Off)
You're a fucking clown, Alan.

Alan sees that Pat is sitting on a bench 10 yards away, just watching him.

ALAN
Oh, hi, Pat.

Pat gets up and advances on him.*

PAT
I trusted you, Alan. I thought we were friends, but you let me down.

ALAN
Well, I, I …

PAT
You got me sacked.

MICHAEL
Over here! Pat, look!

They all turn to look back down the pier. They see Michael is standing on the railings of the pier.

....

* We shot on the pier for two days. It was about minus 12 degrees. That's the glamour of the movies, ladies and gentlemen.

MICHAEL (CONT'D)
Quickly. Look over here!

He hurls himself over the side of the pier.

MICHAEL (CONT'D)
Oh, shit!

There's a splash as he hits the water. Pause.

PAT
What was that?

ALAN
I think it was supposed to be some sort of
distraction, yes. Brave but pointless.

OLD MAN
(Off)
Excuse me.

Three old people stand in the doorway.

ALAN
Oh, God, get back inside, quick, now!

OLD MAN
We want to get down there.

PAT
Do you mind? This is an armed stand-off! Where were
we?

ALAN
I got you sacked.

PAT
Yes, you let me down.

Martin, now on the pier, shouts over his megaphone.

MARTIN
Pat, listen to me!

ALAN
I've got this.

MARTIN
Pardon?

ALAN
I said I've got this.

OLD MAN
How long is it going to go on for?

PAT
Shut up!

OLD MAN
(To his wife)
He's telling you to shut up.

MARTIN
(Indecipherable)

ALAN
Couldn't even get that, it's too close to your
mouth!

MARTIN
(Indecipherable)

ALAN
It's too close to your mouth!

OLD MAN
Did you get that?

ALAN
Did I get what?

OLD MAN
She's saying that if you put your air rifles back
you won't be in too much trouble.

PAT
This is a shotgun.

ALAN
This is an air rifle. That's a shotgun.

OLD MAN
We'll leave you to it.

The old man shuts the door and Alan puts his gun down.

```
ALAN
I surrender.*
```

But Pat has become distant.

```
ALAN (CONT'D)
Pat? Pat?
```

```
PAT
I brought Molly to this pier.
```

```
ALAN
Happy times.
```

```
PAT
I scattered her ashes here.†
```

....

* Alan never actually said this line on the day. We added it in post-production (one of numerous times we added a line in post-production either to add a joke or to smooth over a cut). In this case we'd got rid of a whole chunk in which Alan likened himself to Nazi rocket scientist Wernher von Braun, as someone whose bad deed (betraying Pat/designing Nazi missiles) was surely superseded by a good deed (sticking it to Gordale/helping NASA get to the moon). It slowed it all down and was one Nazi reference too many.

† We'd originally written Pat as a far more cuddly character, to make it more of a turnaround when he snapped and walked into the radio station with a gun. But Colm Meaney brought a harder edge to the character, which was far better. It made his threat more real, which helped Alan's comedy. In this scene, though, Colm showed Pat as a broken, vulnerable man; someone whose life had fallen apart when he'd lost his wife. Pure class from the big Irishman.

ALAN
Oh.

PAT
Buried at sea.

ALAN
Like bin Laden.

PAT
And now here we are, the circle of life.

ALAN
'Cirque de Soleil'.

Pat takes half a pace towards Alan. There's steel in his voice.

PAT
Turn your head away.

MARTIN
Okay, let's calm down.

PAT
Turn your head away.

MARTIN
Pat, listen to me.

ALAN
Pat, you're scaring me.

PAT
I won't ask again.

MARTIN
Pat, I need you to stay calm.

PAT
Turn your head away.

ALAN
(Singing)
'Maybe I didn't love you, quite as often as I could
have …'

PAT
What are you doing?

ALAN
(Singing)
'Maybe I didn't treat you, quite as good as I
should have …'

PAT
Stop it!

ALAN
(Singing)
'And if I made you feel second best, girl I'm sorry
I was blind, 'cause you were always on my mind, you
were always on my mind.'

Alan takes a breath to launch into verse two.

ALAN (CONT'D)
(Singing)
'Maybe I …'

MARTIN
Pat, I need you to keep calm …

ALAN
Shut up, you dick!

Alan turns back to see Pat putting the shotgun into his mouth.

ALAN (CONT'D)
Pat, what are you doing?

Pat replies but it's muffled by the gun in his mouth.

ALAN (CONT'D)
What?

PAT
(Removing the gun)
I want to be with Molly.

ALAN
Pat, don't do this!

MARTIN
Pat, don't do this!

ALAN
(To himself)
Unbelievable.

PAT
I can't reach the trigger.

He turns to Alan.

PAT (CONT'D)
Would you do it for me?

ALAN
Yes, of course I will, mate. Of course I will.

Pat hands him the gun.

ALAN (CONT'D)
It's over, Pat.

Pat looks up as Alan hurls the shotgun up, away and over the edge of the pier.

ALAN (CONT'D)
No more hurting.

But the gun clanks on the railings and goes off, hitting Alan in the leg.

ALAN (CONT'D)
Owwwwww!!!!!

Suddenly there's panic. Alan is hit again near his heart, this time by an armed officer, in slo-mo.

    ALAN (CONT'D)
    You fucking idiot!

He falls over.

EXT. START OF PIER - DAY 4

Don looks up from his gun and realises what he's done.

    DON
    Shit!

EXT. PIER END - DAY 4

Alan lies on the ground. Cops are all over the place. In the confusion, Lynn gets through, reaches Alan and cradles his head as the old people gather round. Cut between their POV looking down at Alan and his POV looking up at them.

    LYNN
    Stay with me, Alan. Stay with me!

    ALAN
    They've blown me to bits, Lynn. I feel cold.

    LYNN
    It's all right, Alan. God is with us.

ALAN
We had some mad times, didn't we, Lynn? There's
some blood coming from my mouth, Lynn.

LYNN
It's just spit.

He investigates with his tongue.

ALAN
Is it? Oh, yes.

PAT
Alan, I'm really sorry.

*A wide shot shows Pat is looking over him with
concern.*

ALAN
It's all right, Pat. I'll — He's still got the gun!

*At that moment, Pat is clattered by onrushing
policemen and disappears from view.*

ALAN (CONT'D)
Was I a good man, Lynn? Was I a kind man?

LYNN
Very kind. I remember when you were defrosting your
freezer and you gave me all that bacon.*

ALAN
I'm ready, Lynn. I think I'm ready.

A seagull lands on his leg. Alan lifts his head up.

....

* This deathbed conversation with Lynn was originally a lot longer. But
when we came to cut down the initial, long cut of the film, Armando
Iannucci felt this scene in particular was outstaying its welcome and
dragging the pace down. As always, he was right. It had to be cut down,
but we lost some good lines in the process.

ALAN: 'Lynn, I do believe in God. And I believe Jesus did all those
things they said he did.'

LYNN: 'Alan, please try to …'

ALAN: 'No, Lynn. I'm sorry for saying he only walked on water
because of a thin layer of ice just below the surface. I also regret
suggesting it was some sort of submerged jetty. That was hurtful.'

ALAN (CONT'D)
Hello, Mr Seagull. Have you come to take my spirit
away?* Go, gull! Gull, gull! Gull ...

*He runs out of breath. As the gull flies up and away,
Alan's head lolls back, eyes open, staring. Lynn gasps
and looks to be in shock. She bows her head, then
reaches over and closes his eyes for him.*

....

* We wanted the film to have a bit of heart and deliberately didn't shy away from emotion in this scene. Pat wasn't an evil man, he'd just been left behind by the modern world. Alan wasn't totally and irretrievably selfish. And Lynn needed to be reconciled with the most important man in her life before he died. That said, we did need to undercut it all with a laugh. The reveal that Alan is just watching the seagull fly away did that for us. It popped the tension that had built up. That said, getting the seagull was one of the toughest battles we had to fight. The production team had major reservations that it would be worth the effort. The main issue was how to get a gull to land on Alan. Doing it on location would be more or less impossible to engineer. In the end, a charity for injured seagulls was tracked down and their finest gull driven to our set in Mitcham, where it was filmed against green screen landing on the legs of Gordon Seed, our Alan stunt double. To be honest, the gull was a bit of a fucking prima donna, but we got there in the end. Its handler was throwing bits of fish onto Gordon's legs to entice the bird. It got greedy, though (gulls, eh?), and vomited up a bellyful of sardines. We originally kept that moment in. Alan had been reverential towards the bird, seeing it as some sort of angel ('Have you come to take my spirit away?'), but then it vomited and Alan snapped out of it, balling the bird out – 'You fucking dirty get!' We removed it in the end. Alan's 'watching it fly away' line should be what punctures the moment. You can't really do it twice. (The line also sounded more like Paul Calf than Alan Partridge.)

ALAN PARTRIDGE: ALPHA PAPA

ALAN (CONT'D)
What are you doing? I'm watching it fly off!

He looks at her properly.

ALAN (CONT'D)
It's weird, Lynn. Yours will be the last face I
ever see.

She smiles. A female PARAMEDIC leans over.*

ALAN (CONT'D)
Oh, good.

PARAMEDIC
Hi there. You're going to be okay.

ALAN
I've been shot in the heart.

PARAMEDIC
Your heart's there. That's your shoulder.

ALAN
(Touching the wound)
No, that, that's my heart. Ow!

....

* The woman playing the paramedic is actually Steve's manager, Anna
Stockton. We needed someone to step in at the very last minute and she
was the fall guy.

LYNN
Can I have my job back now?

ALAN
Yeah, if you want.

Lynn smiles and we see the pier from above. Alan being tended to, Pat being led away. From this distance, we hear Alan's chat.

ALAN (CONT'D)
How long have you been a paramedic?

PARAMEDIC
About four years.

ALAN
Right, and do you start in St John's Ambulance and then work your way up, or are they separate organisations?

LYNN
They're separate organisations.

ALAN
She can answer for herself, Lynn!

PARAMEDIC
They are separate organisations.

ALAN
Right. And are you courting at the moment?

LYNN
Well …

ALAN
Not you, Lynn!

INT. NORTH NORFOLK DIGITAL – FRIDAY – DAY 5
(WEEKS LATER)

*In a mirror of the first scene, the camera comes along
the corridor, and we hear the broadcast before we see
it. It goes past the photos, but Pat and Danny are
missing. Bruno Brookes is there in Pat's place.* *

*JINGLE: 'North Norfolk Digital, North Norfolk's best
music mix.'*

ALAN
(Off)
We've had a letter from Louise, in Thetford, who
says I'm sick to the back teeth of people poking
fun at garden gnomes. They may be small and
strange-faced, but they bring a lot of pleasure to
a lot of people.

....

* In most cases we tried to use cultural references that could be
understood internationally, without compromising the Alan-ness of the
film. In this case we just decided to ignore that and use Bruno Brookes.

INT. RADIO STATION - STUDIO - DAY 5

ALAN
Now that's a letter once upon a time I would have
found offensively dull, but not now.

SIMON
So, maybe everything that happened has changed you.

ALAN
I think I have changed a little bit.

SIMON
Well, for my part, I was a bit worried about my
head … but I think I've got a handle on it now.

ALAN
Oh, yes, that's a good joke.

Alan puts on the travel news. They're off-air.

ALAN (CONT'D)
You've used that joke about three or four times
now. I don't know if you're aware of that?

SIMON
You think I use it too much?

ALAN
I wouldn't say that, I just think we're in that
area, you know …

SIMON
What about the hat?

ALAN
Good for the bin, I reckon.

SIMON
Lose it?

ALAN
Yes. But I think, like I say, you're coming on
leaps and bounds, and I think, you know, in 12
months' time, you'll probably have forgotten there
ever was a siege.

SIMON
(Weakly)
What siege?

ALAN
Exactly! That's good. But you haven't really
forgotten, have you?

SIMON
No.

They're back on-air.

ALAN
Okay, time now for our regular weekly phone call
with incarcerated DJ, Pat Farrell. It's …

STING: 'Ring ring from Sing Sing!'

ALAN (CONT'D)
Hello, Pat! Wha' gwan?

PAT
Hi, Alan.

ALAN
Okay, this week's question comes from Sue, a dental hygienist from Grantham. She asks: prison time is often referred to as porridge, but, she says, do they actually serve porridge and, if so, is it compulsory?

PAT
Well, yes, they serve porridge, but you can have other things …

ALAN
Thanks, Pat. We'll have another question for you next week. Until then …

STING: [Cockney] 'Keep your nose clean, boy.'*

MUSIC: 'The Number One Song in Heaven' by Sparks.

....

* Like a lot of the jingles, this one was performed by Steve 'Man of Many Voices' Coogan. Rob Brydon was unavailable.

INT. PRISON – DAY 5

Pat hangs up the phone with a sigh and walks back to his cell.

BLACK SCREEN

A caption says: 'Pat Farrell featured on Alan's show every week for five weeks. He now writes to Alan once a month and has received one reply.'

EXT. NORFOLK COUNTRYSIDE – DAY 5

Alan is driving a new Range Rover.

BLACK SCREEN

A photo of Lynn.

A caption says: 'Lynn Benfield acknowledges that she developed ideas "above her station" but has since resolved to wind her neck in.

'Alan Partridge now considers the matter closed.'

EXT. NORFOLK COUNTRYSIDE – DAY 5

Alan still driving. We see that Angela is next to him in the passenger seat.

ALAN PARTRIDGE: ALPHA PAPA

BLACK SCREEN

A photo of Michael.

*Caption: 'The emergency services called off the search
for Michael the Geordie after almost 45 minutes.*

'He was never found.'

EXT. NORFOLK COUNTRYSIDE - DAY 5

*Alan looks in the rear-view mirror at Angela's two
teenage boys in the back and shakes his head with a
smile.*

BLACK SCREEN

A photo of Connor.

*A caption says: 'Formed in 1979, Marillion have sold
over 15 million albums worldwide.'*

EXT. NORFOLK COUNTRYSIDE - DAY 5

*The camera pulls back to show Alan's Range Rover is
towing a speedboat named 'Alpha Papa'.*

As it drives away, we hear Alan speak.

ALAN
Colby, Philip. If you guys don't dig the sounds,
sling us your Pod, I'll dock it.

ANGELA'S SON
You won't like it.

ALAN
Guys, I dig a lot of stuff. A good beat's a good
beat.

CREDITS

Music: 'All the Wrong Places' by Example. For about 30 seconds …

ALAN
Sorry, not listening to that.

He puts Sparks back on. Another 30 seconds …

ALAN (CONT'D)
For God's sake, if it's that important!

He puts Example back on. Another 30 seconds …

ALAN (CONT'D)
Sorry, but that is <u>awful</u>.

He puts Sparks back on.

EXT. COUNTRY ROAD – POST-CREDITS

We're back with Alan in the Range Rover. Angela turns to him.

ANGELA
(Pat's voice)
You're not going to believe this.

ALAN
Have you got a cold?

                                        CUT TO:

INT. RADIO STATION – STORE ROOM – DAY 3

Alan is standing by the store room. He's back at the moment he had his first daydream, with Pat looking for the Willie Nelson record. Pat emerges with the photo of the bus.

PAT
It's the old roadshow bus!

Alan tries to get his bearings. He looks perturbed.

ALAN
How long have I been standing here?

PAT
Two or three minutes.

ALAN
Did I leave the radio station for a day and then
come back …?

PAT
No.

ALAN
With pizzas?

PAT
What pizzas?

ALAN
Ohhhh, this is a colossal waste of time! So the
whole … the pier at Cromer? And the black
background with the writing on about what people
were doing …?

PAT
Are you on something?

*External shot of the building. The camera pulls away,
leaving the siege to continue without us.*

```
ALAN
This is fucking ridiculous! I think I'm having some
sort of breakdown.*
```

....

* This was definitely the scene that caused the most arguments. Was revealing the second half of the film to be a daydream a bit of a let down after all you'd been through with Alan, or was it a funny final twist? Did Alan addressing the fact it was a ridiculous waste of time take the curse off it, or was it still a cheat? It was in and out of various cuts right up until the final moment. We even had a version in which we stayed with the scene until you see Alan come out of character and become Steve again. People were split on that one, too. In the end we settled it with a simple fist fight.

ALSO AVAILABLE

'Brilliantly witty'
The Times